"Let your

Best

Dawn.

DECISION

THE GATEWAY TO YOUR UNLIMITED POTENTIAL

First Published in 2024

Success in Doing Publications

Copyright © Donna Kennedy, 2024

The author asserts all moral rights.

ISBN: 978-1-9160176-9-6

www.donnakennedy.com

CONTENTS

INTRODUCTION

The Gateway to Your Unlimited Potential

Unlocking the gateway to your potential, imagine that for a moment — what would that mean for you? What could that do for you? A cascade of possibilities and opportunities, propelling you towards new realities you may have never before imagined. New pathways to success and fulfilment that you thought were unattainable. Embracing change with a new sense of confidence, knowing that your creativity, curiosity and determination have no bounds. Wouldn't that be amazing? It can be! It all starts with a decision.

Decision is the force that changes and shapes destinies and the pivotal moments where the future is sculpted, and the essence of character is revealed. Each choice, no matter how seemingly inconsequential, contributes to the intricate pattern of our lives. It is through the power of decision-making that we mould the clay of our potential and sculpt the masterpiece of our personal transformation and growth.

In this book you will read real-life stories that will show you just how powerful and transformative decisions can be. Stories have always been the vessels of human wisdom, carrying the experiences, struggles, and triumphs of individuals across time and space, and this book serves as a potent elixir, offering invaluable insights and catalyzing transformative change, no matter what your current circumstances are.

The struggles, joys, and challenges portrayed in the narratives here can act as windows into diverse human experiences that can bridge understanding, enabling us to grasp perspectives and emotions beyond our own.

The narratives of the authors function as both mirrors and prisms. They reflect aspects of identity, mirroring fears, aspirations, and challenges. Simultaneously, they refract diverse experiences, breaking it into a spectrum of possibilities for personal growth. These real-life stories can help you to consider alternative paths for growth that you may never have thought of. You will read stories of individuals who overcame adversity, pursued their passions, and experienced profound personal development, by unlocking their limits through decision. The challenges, achievements and triumphs of others can instil a sense of hope and motivation, demonstrating that transformation is not only possible, it's a shared human experience.

Life is a series of crossroads, and at each juncture, we stand before a myriad of possibilities. The power of making decisions lies in our ability to choose our direction deliberately. Every decision, whether small or monumental, propels us along a particular path, steering the course of our journey. The transformative magic happens when we acknowledge and embrace ourselves— the power to act and shape our lives. We are not passive bystanders in life; we can write our own script. By making conscious decisions, we can reclaim control and create a future and life we love.

Decisions are a declaration of our capacity to direct the course of our lives, and this realization is a liberating force. It unlocks the gateway to possibilities. Seemingly small decisions can sprout into monumental transformations, and it is through decision-making that we forge the tools of self-discovery, resilience, and adaptability.

When we consciously make decisions aligned with our values and aspirations, we cultivate an environment conducive to growth. Each decision becomes a stepping stone, paving the way for a more authentic, fulfilled version of ourselves. In this way, decision-making becomes the catalyst that propels us towards our highest potential. It is not solely in the act itself but also in the reflection that follows.

Every decision, whether favourable or challenging, carries lessons, and reflecting on our choices enables us to gain insights into our motivations, fears, and desires, and the wisdom gained from introspection can fuel personal growth. It transforms decisions into valuable experiences, shaping character and refining understanding of who we are.

The power of decision is most evident in the face of uncertainty. Life is fraught with ambiguity and uncertainty, and it is our decisions that serve as the navigational tools guiding us through the unknown. The ability to make decisions, even in the absence of complete information, is a testament to human resilience and adaptability.

The power of decision is intertwined with the courage to choose — the courage to step into the unknown, the courage to challenge the status quo, and the courage to redefine ourselves, even when afraid or uncertain. But it is through this courage that we break free from the constraints of familiarity and embrace the transformative potential of the unknown. It is through the courage to decide that we confront fears, overcome obstacles, and unlock the doors to possibilities.

To harness the power of decision is to recognize the power within yourself. It is a call to be intentional in your choices, whilst aware of the consequences they carry. By embracing the responsibility that comes with decision-making, you can unlock your potential.

Imagine how amazing that will be.

Donna & Pat

CHAPTER 1

LIVE Fully

by Donna Kennedy

I was 14. My body felt like led slumped heavily into the mattress beneath me. My eyes were closed, heavy in darkness. I couldn't open them. I tried to move with every ounce of my being – nothing. I was stuck. I tried calling out – nothing, my mouth wouldn't even open for my voice to surface. An intense fear came over me, a fear that I had never felt before, and with it a horrible realization, *'Had I gone too far? Am I dead? No, I couldn't be dead, I don't want to be dead. I'm in control!'* I desperately tried to move, and with the realization that it wasn't happening, the fear grew, so much and so fast that it felt like a monster coming at me ready to engulf me, and I had nowhere to run. I was completely stuck in my mind. *'I'm not in control of this anymore. I need you to move. Body, please wake up!'*

The sound of the little white alarm clock ticking on my bedside cabinet filled me with absolute panic. No matter how much I willed my body to move, it wasn't going to happen, and time was ticking — literally. Then bizarrely, I settled into calm. I slid into a mind space that I can only describe as numb silence. *'I could just stop trying now, it would be easier to let go. If I stop trying, I could just slip away, and I don't have to exist in the torment of the last few years. Maybe my body is done trying and is now dying? I could just surrender...'*

I was fully aware that on one hand, life was desperately fighting for me and I for it, yet on the other nothingness was happy to take me away. Honestly, in that moment I could have chosen either and going to sleep into nothing seemed to be the easier option. I didn't want to die but I didn't have the energy to fight anymore. So, as I began to shut down in my mind, I prepared in acceptance to drift off, just as you drift into sleep when you go to bed at night. I was deflating, surrendering, giving up. And then the most unusual thing happened.

I began to feel an inexplicable peaceful sensation almost as though something was intervening between me and the silence I was surrendering to. It wasn't a physical touch, external voice, or anything miraculous, but it didn't feel like just me, it was something more powerful and greater than me. It was unusually familiar, and it was like it was speaking to my heart. It was a feeling of pure love and much stronger than any struggle I could ever or have ever gone through. I don't have words to describe it exactly as I felt it, but I was certainly connected to it. No fear, just pure love, total acceptance, and an encouragement I knew I could trust completely, *"Donna, stay awake. Focus Donna."*

And with that I slowly began to feel a glimmer of hope to fight for my life again. It wasn't an enthusiastic surge of energy, but I was holding on. I know with every fiber of my being *that* something breathed life into me again that day, just as I was just about to exhale away. I don't believe I died or had that light-filled near-death experience that other people talk about, but I do believe I was helped to stay connected to life somehow, and I did. Eventually, I managed to open my eyes.

Exhausted, I just lay there, feeling numb at first and then it was like an emotional flood gate opened. I cried, and cried, and cried, thinking everything and nothing at the same time. I couldn't stop the tears flowing.

After I don't know how long, my mother came into my room, and I pleaded for help. I had reached rock bottom, and I didn't know how to get better, but I hoped she might, if I let her. Her response wasn't exactly reassuring. She told me that she didn't know how to help me get better – nobody did.

Then it all came out. I told her I thought I had been secretly in control all this time, but I surrendered to the fact I was not. Ironically, I was completely out of control. I told her that I had been hiding food, so I didn't have to eat it, weighing myself incessantly, over exercising, obsessing over calories, and living on a knife edge between life and death, an edge that I thought I had full control over.

Having plummeted to a weight of 5 stone and being 5'10" in height, it turned out it wasn't a secret I could hide, but I thought I had hidden it by wearing baggy clothes and withdrawing from people around me. It seemed my family were very aware of the danger I had put myself in; they had watched me waste away, watching from the sideline not being able to do anything about it. I was in my own bubble and couldn't connect to their reason or logic. I had ignored them. Despite their persistent efforts, I refused to stop starving myself, and I was on a rapid downward anorexic slope. I had cut myself off and shut myself down, but that day I poured my soul out to my mother in absolute desperation. Everything came out, even things I had tried to bury.

I told her how I had been sexually assaulted when I was 7, and how it felt too big for my brain to handle. She told me that my family knew that something was wrong, although they didn't know what exactly. They had noticed how my happy demeanor had suddenly changed and that I had become withdrawn. I certainly wasn't allowing anyone to know why, it was too much. I was also being bullied at school at the time, which compounded the situation.

It felt like my world was spinning, spinning out of control, and I didn't know how to stop it. It felt like a monster chewing me up and spitting me out – quite literally I suppose. However, I realized that day that despite it all, it was no longer something I could manage on my own. It was a matter of letting people help me or dying. They were my two very real options and only I could decide which route to take.

It wasn't easy but I made the decision to stay connected to life, even though I had no idea how to get better or if I ever could. I just knew that I had to trust and let people help me in any way possible. I needed them to help me carry the weight I had been carrying in my mind, in hindsight weight I had been stripping from my body.

The decision to connect to life and to allow people to help me was a catalyst for many decisions to follow and ultimately my full recovery. It wasn't a flip-the-switch-and-all-is-well magical process, it was very much a case of making moment-to-moment decisions as consistently as possible, and each life-giving positive decision I made and trusted gave me power for the next one. Life is, after all, a series of moment-to-moment decisions. What we do in this moment affects the next, and what we do in the next moment affects the one to follow. Thankfully, the power of consistent decision has got me to where I am today; a healthy, successful and happy woman who now LIVES fully!

There are so many details I could go into about my journey and recovery, but for the purpose of this book, I would like to gift you something that I feel will be of extra value to you in this moment, and that is what I learned life truly is and how to connect with it, so you can LIVE FULLY!

Admittedly, I wasted a chunk of my lifetime, trading it for thoughts, experiences and behaviors that didn't serve me or add value to anything or anyone. My wish for you reading this book is that you don't do the same. I want you to LIVE your life fully from this day on, and not waste a single moment on anything that doesn't bring you value. I will explain why this is so important and how it can be so impactful on your life but before I do, I'd like you to consider this scenario:

Let's take an average 40-year-old person with an average life expectancy of 85 years. At 40 the person will have already lived almost half of their lifetime, leaving them with 16,425 days left to live. Bear in mind that the average person will spend a third of that time (5475 days) sleeping, and a third (5475 days) working. Based on that calculation, it means that an average 40-year-old with a life expectancy of 85 years has just 5475 days left to spend time doing things that they really *want* to do!

This calculation is not intended to scare you, but having the facts placed in front of you like this might be the wake-up call to review the value you are placing on your lifetime and on yourself, and to reflect on the decisions you are currently making in your life.

You see, every day we do lifetime transactions; you trade time for experiences, people, conversations, thoughts, behaviors etc. But if you thought about your life with a new finely tuned awareness of it being time-limited, would you trade your time the way you have been or would you make different decisions? Those experiences you won't let go of, those negative conversations you get caught in, the stuff you expose yourself to day-after-day, the behaviours you engage in, the thoughts you entertain, the phone calls you feel obliged to answer and the people you feel obliged to please etc., would you do things differently and make different decisions if you cherished every moment of LIFE-time?

You see, I have learned that time is our most valuable asset, and it is up to each one of us to decide what to do with it and how we trade it. Life experiences happen that are sometimes not within our control, but how we react to what happens and the decisions we make thereafter will ultimately determine how we live and the quality of our lifetime. Your power to LIVE is in the decisions you make. Some decisions may be easy, and some may be difficult, but your decisions create your life.

My wish for you is that you connect to life and truly LIVE, because having gone through the tough times and come out the other side, I know with confidence the possibilities and opportunities living fully can bring for you. What if there is something more for you in your life? What if your purpose and meaning are bigger than you initially thought? What if you reached more of your potential? Would your decisions be different to the ones you have been making? Begin to open your mind to these possibilities.

In my experience, there are four main components to connecting to life and living fully. I invite you to reflect on them here to see how they might best resonate with you.

LIVE

Love, **I**nspiration, **V**alue, **E**nlightenment.

Love

Firstly, let's look at the dictionary definition of love, which is "a feeling of deep affection." On the surface, it may seem a bit silly to think someone would need love to live fully, but if we look at it a little deeper, you'll see that you actually do, even at the level of basic survival, and its absence or presence influences every decision we make. Of course, love can be present in many forms, but we come into the world innately knowing that it is a necessary component. A newborn baby knows from day dot that it must create a loving bond with their mother or caregiver, if they are to be fed and survive. It cries to get what it needs and when it gets it, it shows a bond-strengthening smile or goo-gah to solidify a loving relationship. That knowing doesn't stop at the baby stage; it continues through our entire lifetime, albeit in different ways.

As babies grow into children, they look for loving reassurance from parents and other adults, later from friends, and then in adult life from a partner, companion, or society as a whole. Without love at some level the human species would not have grown. What's more,

12

studies have shown that the love we feel from those around us can affect us so much that we are neurologically and chemically influenced by its presence or absence. Hundreds of studies have shown that people who do not feel loved and connected to others or validated and accepted are not as happy as those who are and do not behave in the same way. On the flip side, if you consider people who are completely rejected into isolation (the opposite of love), they can become depressed very quickly, sometimes even psychotic. Isolation is a form of torture in some countries! That said, humans need love to survive and thrive. It is not just something we desire. However, and you may not have thought about this, it must start with self-love and self-acceptance.

Without self-love and self-acceptance, it is not possible to fully accept love from others. If you think about it, it was my lack of self-love that led me to push people away and resulted in an existence of misery. I had people around me who loved me, but because I had no self-love, I stayed in my emotional bubble and closed myself off to everyone and any possibility of embracing love in my life. But the importance of loving and accepting yourself cannot be overstated. You must learn to let go of what holds you back and let love and acceptance move you forward with joy and ease.

Letting go and letting love is the most profound act you can ever do, for yourself and others. It has the power to free you from emotional burdens and create space for growth, inner peace and success of all types. While it may seem difficult to do at times, letting go of things that don't serve you is essential for self-love and acceptance. So, as of today, and as you read this book, see it as an intentional act for the purpose of living fully and making decisions that help you succeed. This means respectfully letting go of bad memories, resentment, anger, guilt and grudges and allowing for something better. It's not about being flippant or forgetting, it's getting unstuck, taking back your power and having ownership of your life, intentionally respecting your experiences for all they are, and letting go of what doesn't help you move forward.

Holding on to negativity keeps you trapped in a cycle of negativity. When you choose to release negative emotions you experience freedom, lightness, and emotional well-being, opening the door to new potential on every level, so you can develop a renewed sense of positivity and possibility. It cultivates empathy, understanding, and compassion. It moves you from a space of rumination, resentment and regret to a space for reconciliation and deeper connection with yourself and others, fostering harmonious bonds with love. It is an empowering act that allows you to reclaim control over your direction. By choosing to let go and let love, you can break a victim mentality and take charge of your emotional state. It is a testament to your strength and resilience, reminding you that you have the power to shape your life. The benefits this brings to your mental, emotional and physical well-being are immeasurable!

Inspiration

The word inspiration comes from the Latin word *inspiratus* (the past participle of *inspirare*), which means "to breathe into" and in English has had the meaning "the drawing of air into the lungs" since the middle of the 16th century. When I was ill, I was breathing oxygen into my lungs to exist, but I didn't *feel alive*. Looking back, I truly believe that what kept me alive in my most desperate moments wasn't oxygen, it was inspiration; something greater than me was inspiring me to fight.

I have since come to understand that in the tapestry of life, inspiration weaves the threads that transforms existence into the extraordinary. It is the spark that ignites potential, and the force that propels us towards fulfilment.

At its core, inspiration is the oxygen for the soul, it is the heartbeat of life, the fuel that propels us forward on our unique paths. It breathes life into our aspirations, providing the motivation to reach beyond our perceived limits, and without it we risk drifting aimlessly, disconnected from the core of our being.

Inspiration is the compass that points us towards fulfilment, urging us to pursue our potential and align with our true selves. It breaks down defensive barriers, allowing the mind to be open to and explore uncharted territories, even when you are scared or uncertain. Life has challenges, and inspiration serves as the

15

formidable ally in navigating those challenges, by kindling resilience and reminding us of our intrinsic capabilities to overcome obstacles.

Ultimately, a life devoid of inspiration risks becoming a mere existence, as was mine. To live a life fully, you must make the decision to actively seek and embrace inspiration. It is not a fleeting emotion but a mindset, a conscious decision to engage with the world with open eyes and an open heart. It is my experience that through this intentional pursuit of inspiration, we can sculpt a life that resonates with purpose, passion, and a great sense of accomplishment.

Let me ask you this, when was the last time you intentionally inspired your life? When was the last time you breathed into what's important to you? When was the last time you created or did something for the first time, that you made the decision and committed to energizing your potential with a bigger-picture goal and vision, that you learned something new, so you could challenge yourself, develop and grow intellectually, emotionally, physically, or spiritually? *Now* is a great time to start. Your power is in your decision to LIVE, to value your lifetime and inspire each moment of it going forward, for time is not a given, it is a privilege.

Valuing Time
Time is the currency we all possess in equal measure. Yet, how we spend this invaluable resource determines the trajectory of our

lives. Understanding and valuing time is akin to unlocking the secret code to success, fulfilment, and a life well-lived. Time is a finite resource; once spent, it cannot be replenished. And when you have an awareness of its scarcity it is a reminder to trade your time wisely. In the pursuit of life fulfilment, recognizing that every second is an opportunity for growth becomes paramount. Whether it's filtering your life from negativity, learning new skills, fostering meaningful relationships, or pursuing something you are passion about, each moment offers a chance to contribute to your self-improvement.

When you learn to value time the decision to set clear priorities and goals is inevitable. In a world filled with distractions, it's easy to get swept away by the current of urgency rather than navigating towards what truly matters to you. As you prioritize personal growth, the positive effects ripple through every facet of your life. Time becomes not only a currency for your personal development but also a gift you share with others through meaningful connections and contributions. How are you trading your lifetime? How are you valuing yourself?

It's crucial to remember the intrinsic worth that you carry within yourself. You are unique, special, and irreplaceable, and your journey is unlike anyone else's. Valuing your time and yourself is not an act of arrogance; rather, it's an acknowledgment of your own worth, capabilities, and potential. Just like a rare gem, you possess qualities that make you one of a kind. Your experiences, talents, and the way you navigate the world contribute to the beautiful mosaic of who you are.

Take a moment to reflect on your accomplishments, both big and small, and as you read this book think about how you can appreciate your value and your life more. Isn't it time to celebrate the challenges you've overcome, the lessons you've learned, and the growth you've experienced?

Surround yourself with positivity and people who uplift you. Cultivate self-love and self-care as essential components of your daily routine. Remember that it's okay to set boundaries and prioritize your well-being. You are not selfish for valuing your life and worth; in fact, it allows you to bring your best self to the world. It allows you to live fully!

Your dreams, aspirations, and passions are valid. Your voice matters, and your presence makes a difference. Embrace your uniqueness, be kind to yourself, and never underestimate the impact you have on those around you. You are deserving of love, respect, and all the good things that life has to offer. So, stand tall, be proud of who you are, and never forget the importance of valuing your time. Make the decision to value YOU!

Enlightenment

Enlightenment, often described as a state of profound wisdom, clarity, and spiritual awakening, holds immense importance in life. While enlightenment may have different meanings to different individuals, its essence lies in the pursuit of truth, self-realization, and a deep understanding of the world and ourselves and having faith in that.

Enlightenment can have an impact on every decision you make and every outcome that follows. It offers liberation from the illusions and misconceptions that often cloud our perception of reality. It allows us to see beyond the superficial layers of existence and gain a deeper understanding of the true nature of ourselves and the world around us. By transcending the limitations of ego and attachment, we can free ourselves from suffering, ignorance, and the patterns that hinder personal growth, opening our minds to new possibilities and perspectives. It enables us to see the interconnectedness of all things and understand our place in the larger tapestry of existence. With an expanded consciousness, we become more attuned to the present moment, embracing each experience with a sense of awe and gratitude. It's a conscious moment-to-moment ownership of decisions, leading you to make wiser choices and live a more purposeful and fulfilling life.

When I chose to surrender to my tug-a-war emotional struggles, I found an inner peace and contentment that was not dependent on external circumstances. No matter how bad things were, surrendering helped me to find peace amidst the chaos and uncertainty. Instead of trying to figure everything out myself and not feeling capable of doing so, I could tap into intuition, inner wisdom, and the universal intelligence that guides us all towards our highest potential. By aligning ourselves with a higher consciousness, we unlock our creative abilities and find deeper meaning. You don't have to do things on your own.

Enlightenment is a transformative journey that holds immense importance in life. It offers liberation from illusions, expands consciousness, cultivates inner peace, connects us with higher wisdom, and inspires compassionate action. While enlightenment may be an ongoing process rather than a final destination, its pursuit enriches our lives, elevates our experiences, and brings us closer to the truth of who we are and our purpose in the world, which is ultimately why we are here. You have purpose, your life has meaning, and your life matters more than you may ever comprehend.

Decide to LIVE

Make the decision today to LIVE and you will open the gateway to your unlimited potential. Your goals, your dreams and your greatest desires are all waiting for you. Nobody can live your life better than you. Nobody can be you better than you. Now is your time to step up and make the decision to be all you can be and all that you deserve to be. Today is the first day of the rest of your life. Grasp it and live FULLY!

CHAPTER 2

Out Of Your Depth

by Shaun McLaughlin

It was Wednesday the 18th of May 2022. Finally, I was on the beach in Puerto del Carmen, Lanzarote, with a small group of about a dozen other Irish people. It was a glorious sunny day, not a cloud in the sky and a gentle warm breeze was coming off the Atlantic Ocean. The large beach was busy with holidays makers enjoying the summer sun. The majority of us had travelled over that morning on a flight from Dublin. We were all pulling on wetsuits, zips were being yanked up, some helping others, fixing goggles and swim hats. A stick of anti-chaff was being passed about and anti-fog was being sprayed into goggles to stop them misting up when in the water. All the necessary small final adjustments were being made to our kit before entering the water.

Coming from the very north of Donegal, the heat of the sand on this beach came as quite a shock, as I slid off the flip flops, the sand burning the soles of my feet. I gingerly stowed my clothes and the few personal belongings I had with me away in a small rucksack and placed it on top of a sun lounger that was free, close to the small pile of bags and towels that had now begun to form from the other members of our group. One person who was not going into the water was designated to "stand guard" over our possessions as they enjoyed the now late afternoon sun in an adjacent recliner.

Looking out at the ocean I could already feel a small bit of anxiety starting to creep in and the apprehension beginning to build. Approximately 60 hours later I would be back on the same beach, standing with approximately 2000 other athletes at the start line of the 2022 Ironman Lanzarote. An endurance triathlon race off 140.6 miles in length, starting with a 2.4-mile open water swim, then onto a 112-mile bike section with over 8500 ft of climbing around the windswept volcanic island of Lanzarote and then finally finishing with a marathon distance run of 26.2 miles along the sea front all against the clock.

All the respective disciplines had cut-off time limits set on them, meaning you had to have each event completed inside a certain time window. Failure to reach the end of that particular section meant you would be "pulled" from the race and not allowed to continue and hence not finish the overall race. Each event followed one another, the only break being the small amount of time you took, known as "the transition" to change out of one set of clothes and into the next, all the while consuming some food during the process. Not only was this my first attempt at an Ironman distance triathlon, this was to be my first ever triathlon.

On a circuit consisting of hundreds of Ironman races throughout the world, the Lanzarote Ironman had garnered the reputation of being one of the hardest to do, with its extremely mountainous and hilly bike course around the volcanic island, only made harder by the ever-constant winds coming off the Atlantic Ocean, that made the first half of the race and the majority of the mountain climbs that bit harder. It was definitely seen as the one every self-respecting triathlete should try and with an average DNF (Did Not Finish) rate of approximately 25-30%. The finisher's medal and T-Shirt from this race was a highly coveted prize to cherish and held a certain amount of kudos in the endurance event circle.

Standing on that beach was the culmination off over 7 months dedicated training, with countless 5am starts, trips to the Foyle Arena swimming pool and the Malin Head pier (the most northerly point in Ireland). Countless hours were spent on the turbo trainer in the middle of my kitchen floor, and then on the weekend the long bikes, which typically lasted five to 6 hours around the roads and hills of the Inishowen Peninsula, Donegal, and then followed by hundreds of miles of running on the very same roads.

Standing there I thought about all the sacrifices that were made to get to this point, all the early 5am starts, the now thousands of miles of training miles accrued, the military level planning ahead of my week to ensure that all the training boxes for the next 7 days got ticked off, all the while having to make sure that all the other everyday tasks were done, getting out the door to work and that time was spent with those closest to me. While preparations for this event had taken over my world and pretty much consumed my head space for 7 months, normal life still went on around me.

24

I was abruptly snapped out of my daydream with the voice of my brother, Patrick, as he decided to take charge of the situation, calling out "Right, are we all set?" On his command the troops started to rally, and a degree of organization took over the group. A plan was devised that we would swim out to some yellow buoys that were a few hundred meters out, stopping occasionally. Patrick, a seasoned and well-respected triathlon coach, was in his element surrounded by fellow previous Ironman finishers. He was the reason I was on the island in the first place as this was his stag-do. Originally, he was meant to do this race a few years previously, but with the recent pandemic it kept getting cancelled and rolled over into the next year. So, to kill two birds with the one stone, the trip abroad to the race was combined with the stag do.

As I said earlier, I could already feel a small bit of anxiety welling and a degree of apprehension build as we collectively turned towards the sea and started to wade into the tide. A fair degree of this was accredited to the usual pre-race nerves, which were to be expected in the days before a big event, a feeling I was all too familiar with. Another reason for feeling this and the overriding cause was my deep-rooted fear of water, in particular DEEP WATER.

An event earlier in my life, about 20 years previously, had left a long-lasting impression on me. During a day away with friends I was thrown off a body board by a wave. I got caught in a rip current, pulling me out into the larger waves and deep water, to the point I wasn't able to stand up. I still remembered the feeling of panic that had consumed me back then, at the point when I realized that I could no longer feel the ground underneath my feet and that I was well out of my depth. Things had taken a turn for the worse. What took place after that was about 20 of the most frightening minutes of my life as I struggled with waves and currents in an attempt to make it ashore. It was my "life flashing before your eyes" moment. Obviously, I was able to walk away from that experience with a healthy respect for the sea but also a memory and an association with deep water that would remain with me and locked away for years.

Back to the present day I knew this was a bridge I had to cross at some stage but managed to dodge up until this point. In the 7 months leading up to the race I calculated I had accumulated nearly 60 miles of swimming in my training. When I had started training in earnest back in November of 2021, I could swim but I would not have classed myself as a "swimmer". Twelve lengths of the 25-metre pool in the Foyle Arena, Derry, a total distance of 300 metres, was my limit but over the weeks and months I had managed to build this up to a stage whereby I could undertake the 2.4 miles as required by the event, an achievement that in itself gave me some sense of pride as I walked into the tide, feeling my wetsuit starting to fill with the warm sea water. Throughout my training I clung to the notion that as the old saying goes, "it'll be alright on the night."

We all walked into the tide until the water line was slightly above our waists. By now I could feel the sea water starting to course and permeate through all the voids and empty spaces created by the folds in my wetsuit. I deliberately stayed to the back of the pack, so as not to hinder the group, consisting of well-seasoned triathletes, bar one other fellow newbie, and also in a bid to hide the nerves and apprehension that by now must have been starting to show on my face. Some of those at the front of the group had started to dive in and fully immerse themselves in the water. I hesitantly took another few steps further in, the water creeping to near my chest.

My brother looked back to check where I was, picked up on my reluctance and called back to see if I was alright. I muttered something back about not being too fond of deep water whilst also trying to downplay the uneasiness that was steadily building internally. Another few seconds later everyone had fully entered the water and I was the last to go. Eventually the stage was reached that I either had to get on with it or turn back and so with a blind leap of faith, my heart pounding in my chest, one last check of goggles, I took a deep breath, jumped forward and into the sea. First hurdle overcome — I was now in the water.

My group had already started their swim out to the first buoy. I quickly tried to gather myself, divert my attention to the job at hand and focus my attention on something other than the vastness of the seabed that was starting to open out in front of me. Even though my instinct at this was to take my head up out of the water, I needed to keep my face down, making the body as streamlined as possible, in an attempt to swim at some half decent rate and follow the group. So again, focusing I started into the front crawl, counting every stroke, and turning my head out of the water every 4th stroke and catching a breath. I managed to catch a glimpse of some members of my group ahead and was conscious of the distance of the gap that was already starting to form, which only added to the pressure of the situation.

For my open water swimming, in training I used to swim inside the relative safety of pier walls, in a local fishing port. I would swim from the pier to a line of rocks that formed the opposite side of the bay. One length over and back was approximately 100 metres and all within a safe depth of about few metres and I made sure that never changed, but now this was a totally different scenario. With every stroke I took I was moving forward, but also simultaneously the seabed was beginning to get further away. Within a couple of minutes, the relative safety of the few metres I was used to had gone. I even found myself starting to curse my goggles, though they protected my eyes from the salt water, they gave me a clear view of the world that was now stretched out below me and the vastness of it all. It was only then that the sheer enormity of the open sea struck me and at that moment I could relate to those people who have a fear of large empty spaces. Beautiful and all as it was, I could start to feel those pangs of panic and fear starting to well up and grip me again. The further I went out I eventually reached the stage where even the seabed began to get obscured and disappear into a blue haze as the water depth increased.

Then the flood gates opened, and all the fear, doubts and negative self-talk that I had managed to dodge and keep locked away started to consume my thoughts and wash over me. '*What are you doing here? Did you honestly think you could actually swim 2.4 miles open water swim, never less do an actual Ironman in 3 days? Those other people are "real" athletes and you're just a pretender. Plus, to everyone that knew me, this event and the training, was pretty much all I had talked about for the past six months, what would they think of me, if I couldn't even do the swim event, never mind finishing the race itself?'*

I remember the one overriding feeling was that I had now run out of hiding places and here in the situation I now found myself, out in the middle of the sea with the majority of my group now 20-30 metres ahead of me, out of my depth, being quickly consumed with panic, I had to face the situation head on and start coming up with some solutions pretty sharpish. My swim stroke had now quickened to the point that any semblance of good technique had gone out the window and turned more into an attempt to stay afloat. Plus, the loss of coordination meant a few mouthfuls of sea water were unintentionally inhaled which only added to the fear and the oncoming panic. If ever there was a time or situation that needed evaluation it was now. In amongst all the thoughts and feelings that were swimming around in my head, I knew that if I didn't do something and get a handle on the situation, I could find myself in a situation that was already rapidly spiraling out of control and ultimately, have outright panic ensue. Images of having to be rescued, lifeguards, coast guard helicopters, CPR and hospitals all briefly flashed by in amongst the multitude of other things that were now swirling around in my head. Oh, the irony of it all, an ironman competitor not even able to do a gentle practice swim.

So, here I was less than 3 days out from one of the biggest challenges that I had decided to undertake, on the verge of a panic attack, in deep water and rapidly running out of options. Thankfully, in the recesses of the mind there was still a small voice desperately trying to be heard in amongst the chaos. I had always heard of the "fight or flight" analogy being widely used and this was getting a front row seat seeing it in action, as my survival instincts kicked in. I knew deep down that if I allowed myself to tip over the edge and go to pieces there would be no coming back and I'd may as well throw in the towel there and then. It was at that point I found myself, unconsciously at the start to be honest, mentally reaching out, grappling at all the various pieces and components forming my current situation, in an attempt to start bringing some reason, semblance back into the fray and figure it all out. It was time to steady the ship.

'Right Shaun, you're wearing a wetsuit, that alone is giving you buoyancy...even if you just do nothing you'll float on the surface. Ok, there was one thing I could pin down that was within my control. Great so there was thing number 1...check. Right, you still CAN actually swim, so it's not the lack of ability. It's just the fact you're in deep water and that has gotten into your head.' The realization that I was giving 100% of my attention and focus to the deep water and all the various associations and external factors that I had attached to that was the origin of my immediate predicament. The realization was that in the space of a few minutes I had not suddenly just lost all my ability to swim. Physically I knew that I was still able, even though mentally I was being told otherwise. So, there is number 2...check.

My mental checklist was starting to build. Even these 2 ticks on my list alone gave me enough presence of mind to take a step back from the edge of the abyss, so that all hope was not lost and ultimately bring some calm back into the situation. As the well-used aphorism says, "if you find yourself in a hole, stop digging." So, against every instinctual reaction I was having at the time, I made a conscious decision to slow things down and attempt to bring a bit of order back. I deliberately reduced the pace and tempo of my swim stroke and started to call the time out in my head *1, 2, 3 and breath on 4*, lifting my head out of the water, inhaling, and filling my lungs up again. *1, 2, 3 and breath and repeat*. Even though the thought of the deep water, which I was still very much in, was at the forefront of

31

my mind, I purposely tried not to focus on it too much. The mantra of my swim stroke was now the only show in town, with the that count to 4 now playing on a continuous loop in my head. Even though at this point, without looking up I realized that the main group were probably well ahead but again I knew at some point they'd stop and re-group in a few minutes. *'Just get to them and I'll get a breather.'*

Again, the count to 4 was now a steady rhythm and a quick lift of the head to sight ahead did indeed confirm I was hanging onto the shirt tales of the main group as I spied the small various coloured dots of their swim caps and my brother's pull buoy in the water up ahead.

A further reassessment and the conclusion that I was now moving again, albeit slowly, gave me a bit of a boost. A few minutes later the main group came to a standstill at the first arranged stop just 500 metres from the where we'd started.

Looking back now I also remember the feeling of getting annoyed and irritated at myself. I was always someone who liked physical challenges and pushing the endurance envelope. Since 2004 I had racked up over countless half marathons and forty-plus stand-alone marathon distance events, plus multiple ultra-marathons and endurance events in addition to that.

Some previously completed milestones included The Infamous "Connemara 100", a solo non-stop 100-mile road race through the west of Ireland, "The Quadrathon", an event consisting of four back-to-back marathons done over four consecutive days and a 250-kilometre unsupported multi discipline off-road endurance race with a 24-hour time limit aptly called "The Race." I had plenty of skin in the game and was no stranger to pushing the limits once in a while. I already had evidence rooted from past endeavors and achievements plus I was relatively comfortable with the fact of being uncomfortable for a duration.

Did I question myself? Of course, I did. As I said earlier, I found myself getting annoyed at the fact that previously I had always managed to achieve whatever I had set out to do and now I was facing the prospect that I might have overstepped the mark. A great line from the original Top Gun movie came to mind when Tom Cruise's character, Maverick, was getting a dressing down from one of his senior instructors, "Son, your ego is writing cheques your body can't cash". All of a sudden there was a big immovable roadblock in my path. The fact that I had an event in less than 3 days and here I was facing the reality that I might not be able to start, yet even complete. While it might not have meant a lot to most, I had put everything into getting to this point, all the work, sacrifices, time and effort and what was it for now? Plus, the old "what would everyone one else think" was in there too. One thing that I had learnt from all my previous endurance events was that no matter how fit or physically able you are, if the mind goes and you lose the mental aspect, then it is game over. If the head is not in the zone, unable to muster the mental strength and dig deep when physical discomfort and exhaustion kicks in then you will not last the duration. Plus, this time, it felt different, very different.

Anyone who has stepped onto a start line be that a 5k or a 100-mile race will more than likely have had some pre-race nerves on the day and some apprehension in the days and weeks leading up to their event. All my events in the past had either been on the roads and trails, and any water encountered was always done from the relatively safety of a kayak once you mastered the art of getting it to go straight and in the general direction you wanted. The fact that you were well above the water line and being able to just stop and chill out for a few minutes if needed on a kayak was not lost on me. But this time, it was different, very different and how was I going to get myself out of it.

A few minutes later I managed to catch up with my group who were all by now arranged in a close circle, everyone floating blissfully in the now late afternoon sun, shooting the breeze. I remember thinking of the two very distinct scenarios being played out at the time. Number 1, all the "athletes" being totally relaxed soaking up the atmosphere and Number 2, the inner turmoil going on in my head. My brother checked in with me to see how I was doing, and he picked up on the fact that all was not going well. Even though the break was very welcome in that it gave me an opportunity to gather myself and get my breath back, I was still very aware of the fact that I was still in deep water and now stationary, losing the assistance to float that the swimming gave me. Even though the wetsuit alone gave a good degree of buoyancy, a fact that was pretty much lost on me again, I found it a struggle to keep afloat as I paddled away under the surface, which only added to my growing list of frustrations. My brother suggested pulling my knees into my chest instead, which helped a lot. Again, I took the conscious decision to try and keep calm as I found the anxiety beginning to rise again.

The group then decided to go to the next buoy which would now bring us parallel along the shoreline. *What to do? Return to shore or go again? Give up or press on?* Logic dictated that the water wouldn't be getting any deeper, even though I was probably in twenty-plus metres of depth at this stage now anyway. Uncomfortable and all as I was, I had managed to get this far coupled with a desire not to let this break me I agreed to go to the next buoy and then head for the shore closely shadowed by my brother, and that would do me for the day.

As I made my way back to the beach and seeing the seabed starting to re-appear, the apprehension slowly started to fade as the water depth decreased. We finally made it back to a point where I was able to stop swimming and let my feet settle back onto the sand, solid ground never felt so good. As I took my final few swim strokes, pulling down the neck of my wetsuit to allow it to fill with a large quantity of water, a trick to allow easy removal, I couldn't but help feel totally dejected and downhearted as I walked out of the sea. Our practice swim that day lasted less than 15 minutes, and the swim part of the Ironman was in reality going to take me the best part of two hours to complete. If I was going to let my nerves and apprehension overcome me at the very beginning, how was I ever going to complete the event at all, would I even start? *'Right, how am I going to overcome this one? There has to be a way! You managed to overcome all the other problems encountered in previous events!'* Questions and statements like that consumed and preoccupied my mind for the rest of that day.

There was another organized group swim for early the next morning by a local guide and swim coach from Lanzarote, which would be well attended by other Ironman entrants. I knew deep down that if I was to overcome this fear and attempt to build some sort of confidence, I had to face this problem head on. I decided that at 7.30am the next morning I would be back on that beach and give it another go, and I had that window of time to come up with some sort of a plan to address the problems. There was another member of our group, a runner like me, who had an impressive resume of ultra-distance events under her belt and was undertaking the Ironman event for the first time. She too was not a strong swimmer and was having battles of her own grappling with the task ahead.

Knowing that someone else was in the trenches with me, a point to bounce ideas off, was a big help.

But a question had to be asked, if I was going to rock up to that beach the next morning and potentially put myself through another taxing trial going by that day's experience what was my WHY? Truth be told, the swim that day and all that had happened during it had totally knocked my confidence, that much was clear. Now I had to ask WHY was I going to do it again and if I had the self-belief to be able to handle it if panic started to take hold again. Could I talk myself down from the edge again and keep it together?

To me endurance events like this were always a way whereby I, and anybody else who was willing to push the boundaries, could actually find out what they are truly capable of, both physically and mentally. I always found something wonderful in that feeling of thinking to yourself that you're not going to be able to finish, when the needle is in the red, but then finding something internal where you're able to overcome a challenge, dig deep into your reserves and find out that you're able to do it. On reflection there is always a great sense of pride in finishing and knowing it didn't beat you when you could have so easily just quit.

For me it was more important to give it a shot, my best shot, and fall short rather than walk away not even having tried. It wasn't part of my DNA too not try. I knew if I didn't at least attempt to give it my all, on reflection, I'd be very disappointed in myself and regret not having a go. So, deep down it was ultimately a decision of not having regrets that sealed the deal and ensured I'd be back on the beach the next morning.

During the remainder of the day, I thought back to the many other times that I had come against setbacks, obstacles and previous other experiences when I had to dig deep to get me through hard times in events. I suppose in some way I was trying to rebuild my self-confidence again after the setbacks from earlier in the day. I thought back to when I had done my first half marathon in Omagh in 2004, the exhilaration of cross the finish line, a mixture of delight and exhaustion coupled with thinking how could anyone be able to do that distance again and be able to run a marathon, but later that year I did just that completing the Dublin Marathon in 2004 and repeated on multiple occasions after that throughout the world. Then in 2011 for the first time I heard of a thing called an "ultra" marathon consisting of 39.6 miles, a marathon and a half, surely that wouldn't be possible but low and behold a year later there I was on the start line of that very race and finished it.

A few years later in 2015, my interest spiked again when I saw the "Quadrathon" event, which was incidentally on my front door in Donegal. Four marathons in 4 consecutive days, all one after the other, and another opportunity to push my levels of endurance again. The numbers of miles in the events were now starting to rise.

I particularly recalled some times during the later stages of this event when fatigue had set in, having to set small goals along the roadside in an effort to keep going...the next telegraph pole, the next turn in the road. Literally the last marathon I ran in that event was broken down into hundreds of small goals and targets, again in an attempt to stop being overwhelmed by the task at hand and the big number of miles involved.

On the very last day of the Quadrathon I was on bus to the start line, and I overheard a conversation between two fellow athletes in the seats behind me, about a 100-mile road race that was happening the following week in the west of Ireland called the Connemara 100. Once more, the numbers staggered me, 100 miles in one go, surely that has to be the pinnacle of endurance, who could someone actually do that in one go? But again, two years later there I was standing outside the Clifden Station House in Galway at 6am on an August morning with 18 other hardy souls at the start line of the aforementioned race. Incidentally on that occasion too, it was touch and go up until the final days before that event, if I was going to be able to participate, after picking up an injury in the final few weeks of my training.

I remembered pondering over the same set of questions back then too, thinking about all the time, effort and money I had poured into preparations and training, wondering if it had all been in vain as well. But start it I did, and it was an amazing event with a rollercoaster of emotions that tested me to my absolute limit, both mentally and physically. I used my old trick deployed to such great effect in the Quadrathon a few years previously of mentally breaking down the 100 miles into smaller bite sized chunks — 10 miles by 10 times, which then at times were broken down into even smaller segments when the numbers got too big, and the fatigue was really starting to bite.

My sister who was part of my support crew took a picture of me wrapped in a blanket at 1am in the morning, sitting on a sea wall in the village of Roundstone at the 81-mile checkpoint in the event. By this stage I was on my feet for just a tad over 18 hours and still had 19 miles to go and I was definitely starting to dip into my reserves.

As I sat on the sea wall, wrapped in my duvet for warmth, taking some nutrition onboard I remember the internal battle going on in my head between the need to get going again and just wanting to sit in the heat and warmth of my duvet for another few minutes. The angel on one shoulder saying, "time to back on the road" and the devil saying, "one more minute." As mentioned previously, one of my main go-to tools that I use often and coach my clients to use when undertaking a big event or task, is to mentally break it down. For my 100 miler it was 10 miles by 10 times, and even then, reduced that even more when the need arises. If the 10 miles was too big an ask and it was especially near the end of the event, then it was just the mile in front of me, just get to the next mile and every time the notification went off on my GPS watch to indicate one more completed, it was another small win on my journey.

As Ken Chlouber, founder of the Leadville 100, widely regarded as one of the toughest endurance races in the world said, "Make friends with pain and you'll never be alone". In a roundabout way he says that to achieve any goal of great importance, you have to get comfortable with being uncomfortable. On reflection, I looked back at all my previous achievements and remembered the times when I was definitely experiencing discomfort, but I still pushed myself through the experience to reach the objective on the other side. Sometimes I was able to do it whilst on the move and sometimes I needed to pull up, take 5 minutes time out and then get back on the horse. Mentally, I knew that I was going to experience some discomfort, but what was inside my control and what was outside it? A bit of self-reflection to be better prepared was needed.

- What happened?
- WHY did it happen?
- How can I do better and prepare myself in the future?

What happened was fairly evident at this point. The fear of the deep water had taken hold to the point of consuming me and overriding everything else. It was something that was not going to go away

41

overnight, so I had to come up with some strategy of work around or alongside it.

Why it happened was essentially down to not having practiced swimming in this scenario in my training for the event. While I had put in the hours and miles, that was not in doubt, these were all done in the pool and inside the relative safety of my pier walls. At the back of my mind, I had an inkling that the deep water might be an issue, I pushed it to the back recesses of my psyche with an "It'll be alright on the night" outlook.

Recognition of the fact that I was SOLELY focusing on the deep water and all the connotations that went along with it, was taking away from everything else, and blocking me from all the reasons that were allowing me to reach my goal. In a large part I was getting in my own way to a degree. The quote by Henry Ford, "*Whether you think you can or think you can't – you're right*" rang true.

'*Right, how can I do this better?*', I was identifying the thought process then re-framing it, changing the narrative to a belief and a way of thinking that was more productive and empowering. I had overcome obstacles in the past and I really knew deep down I was physically capable of the task and that it wasn't a case that I was suddenly incapable of swimming. That self-belief in my ability alone, copper-fastened by identifying the sources of confidence from what I had done and achieved in the past, was the mast all my hopes were pinned to. If I could just shift my focus when I was in the water, it would at least give me a fighting chance. If I could just control and stay on top of that! The big light bulb moment was the realization that what I needed was already inside of me and with a bit of work keeping all of it under control, I would be able to steer a path to where I wanted to go. If I could, if I could, now if I could, was the question that hopefully deep down, I would find the answer to when I went back into the sea. So, that night I went to bed with my toolbox packed with strategies:

- Affirmations of positive self-talk to convinced me that I had the skills and abilities needed to see this through. Going back to the Henry Ford quote I was going to make sure the "I can" version of Shaun McLaughlin was the one that was going to turn up at the beach the next morning and on the start line a few days after that.

- My highlight reel and reflection on past success, as I said earlier, was the foundations of my strategy. Recollection of past successes and achievements, and visualisation of how they felt at the time of doing them. The sheer and utter joy of crossing the finish line on the main street in Clifden after completing the Connemara 100 mile. How every joint and muscle ached with pain, but I had just run one hundred miles non-stop, all the doubts and setbacks I had leading up to it but here I was crossing the finish line having achieved it. The

43

process was repeated for all of the other finish lines I had crossed, each one giving me a bit more momentum.

So, next morning it was all down to the beach again. This time a bit wiser but still with a fair degree of apprehension. With the swim early in the morning and the group meeting up at 7am, it was with a larger crowd consisting of many nationalities. A crowd of about seventy to eighty had formed, men and women the majority fit looking, all seasoned ironman athletes some sporting the iconic Ironman logo tattoos on their calf muscles indicating their past race accomplishments and victories.

In our group the usual pre-swim routines observed the day before were played out again, with wet suits being pulled on and zips cords reached for and yanked up. The anti-chaff stick was doing the rounds again which I applied liberally hoping that it was somehow infuse me some mystical soothing and calming effect I badly needed at the time. The local swim coach was giving a talk about tides times, currents, and what to do on race morning to get the maximum benefit of these conditions. I'll be honest I never heard one word of it, I was so wrapped up in my head with the anticipation of what lay ahead. The start button on my plans to help was pressed and all my tools were now being brought out of their box. One thought about how yesterday's swim was easier as ignorance was indeed bliss but now, I had an idea of what awaited me and that wasn't necessarily a good thing. I snapped myself out of it and started to re-shift my focus. I could already feel the anticipation starting to well up in my chest, my breathing getting deeper and the heart rate beginning to rise.

'*Deep breathes, Shaun. Breathe, slow it down, slow it down*', I repeated to myself. I intentionally reduced the rate at which I was breathing which helped stem the trepidation. '*You can do this. You can do this.*' I announced to myself under my breath as the lecture from the local swim coach concluded and the congregation turned and made their way down to the water. I remembered the sand was a lot cooler in the morning than the burning that greeted us the day before.

Into the water we went, the wetsuit slowly starting to fill again, the cue that I had reached the point where my staying power was going to be tested again, the Rubicon was about to be crossed. *How bad do I want this? Is it really worth ALL this bother and hardship? Why am I putting myself through all this again?* More fleeting questions popped into my head with every step. At that moment in time, I don't know if I had answers to all of them. Wading through the water felt like walking through mud, the feet feeling as if they were being weighed and bogged down. '*Snap out of it!*', I was conscious that I didn't want to go too far down that path, I re-shifted my focus back to what I could control. Concentrating on the breathing again I instantly felt a bit more at ease again. I mentally called myself out, issuing a telling off and doubled down on consolidating what was going on between the ears. I knew physically I had it in me and now it was a case of tying it all together. If I could just get to the other side of this, I knew the rewards and sense of accomplishment would be immense. The plan was, while being aware of external observation to just about what was needed to get the job done, the majority of attention would be internal based, broad and narrow. "Broad internal", knowing and executing what I had to do to complete the swim strategy and then "narrow-internal", analyze and adjust, focusing on my breath, rhythm and keeping tensions at bay. By using positive "distractions" my plan was to keep the mind busy for the most part so as to re-direct it somewhere more pleasant. Steering my mind away from the fact I was in deep water and giving it something to do and get into the "flow". I knew from all my previous events that when you achieve the "flow" state, every action, movement and thought follows inevitably from the previous one, hitting the sweet spot and being "in the zone" or the infamous "runner's high". Sounds easy, eh!

As the water came up and up it was eventually time to take the plunge. A large inhale to fill the lungs with air, a dive into the water, which was now nearly up to my chest, and away we go again. The same beautiful sight of the underwater world met me again and it was a wonderful thing to look at. Small shoals of fish darted here and there along with more exotic looking ones that lazily drifted through near the seabed. Being within a few metres of depth, all was still fine inside. I focused on getting into a steady swim stroke as soon as possible and get the mind "locked in" to the time and rhythm. A quick look up just to confirm where my other group members were and seeing my brother pull the buoy just a few metres ahead of me helped settle things down. A quick self-assessment to check my position in the water followed up by a few readjustments helped me feel more athletic, stronger and capable of delivering more powerful purposeful strokes. It was time to go to work, mentally this was my que to open up all the "taps".

I started off by getting my timing right and focusing on the now familiar 1, 2, 3 and breathing on the 4. Again, and again until the count and the feelings were second nature to me. I could feel my body cutting through the water as my outstretched arms went into the sea, my hands and forearms "catching" the water propelling me forward. I was most definitely on the move and also getting into deeper water. As the bottom got further and further away again, I knew I was getting near the point of the previous days' "episode". I doubled down on my efforts to stay mentally focused, but even with my best efforts a few small thoughts started to slip in. *'That's getting deep'*, I heard myself saying, as a few pangs of anxiety started stabbing and taking hold again. From that point on, I knew that I had to acknowledge the fact that I was in deep water, rather than trying to ignore or skirt around the fact. I couldn't do that swim or eventually the race with my eyes closed for the duration so time to knuckle down.

'Right Shaun you're in the middle of it now, this is what you signed up for and you have to own it.' So, with the eyes open, and those few dissenting voices in my head, I resumed my best streamlined position in the water and focused on delivering those powerful, purposeful strokes, calling out the time in my head and flooding my mind with all the positive self-talk I could muster. Every swim stroke was visualized, my hand and forearm going into sea, catching the water and propelling me forward with purpose. I imagined with each stroke, as my arms pushed the water away, me pushing all the negative thoughts, feelings, and emotions down further. While I knew that they were probably not going to go away any time soon I was determined to tame them and keep them at bay as best I could. All the while my mantras of "You can do this" and the word "STRONG", along with the count of 1, 2, 3, 4 ringing in my ears.

So, 40 minutes later and with 1100 metres on the clock I returned to the beach. Whilst not perfect, it was a better showing than the previous day's swim. In myself I knew that I had handled today a lot better and that in itself gave me a bit more confidence and a huge lift. Maybe all hope wasn't lost just yet. Whilst the demons were still there, I had learnt how to handle them more effectively. I chuckled to myself as I came out of the water, undoing the zip on the wetsuit, with a bit of practice, I might even be able to use them to my advantage on race day.

So, next morning there I was back on the beach for one last blast before race day. The purpose of today's exercise was to build on what I had learnt from the day previous. While the swim was shorter as was now only 24 hours from the event itself, I managed to build on the foundations that were now laid. On a scale of 1-10 I was now down to a 5, a long way from the full on 10 I experienced two days previous.

Then the next day at 7.15am, along with nearly 2000 Ironman competitors, I entered the water to start my triathlon journey. Then 1 hour and 50 minutes later I came back out having completed my 2.4-mile open water swim and then onto my bike.

About 12 weeks after that I found myself back on the start line of Ironman Cork, back home in Ireland, taking another 6 minutes off my time from Lanzarote and a finishing time of 13hours 56minutes.

Then again in May 2023 I was back on the same beach in Lanzarote for Ironman number 3. This time I completed the swim in 1hr 34minutes, a full 26 minutes faster than my time 12 months previous. On this occasion I soaked up the atmosphere and as I entered the water, I was a lot more confident and taking great pride in how far I had come. Those feelings I had when I entered the water a year before were not lost on me, but how I had overcome them, and all the strategies used were definitely going to be added to my toolbox, along with all the others, for the next time....and there will be a next time!

CHAPTER 3

The Power of Thought

by Maeve Kelly

I was lost in a body that I could no longer identify with. It felt like I had been abducted, it was almost like someone had opened the crown of my head and pulled every fiber of my being out that I had known for over forty years and replaced it with someone else. My bones were completely broken, and I was afraid to sleep in case I didn't wake up. My heart was broken listening to my daughters scream with night terrors, not being able to run to their rooms to reassure them that they were now safe. Instead, all I could do was lie there in pain and scream their names, in the hope they would wake and come to me; but also knowing that I was a reminder for them of that dreaded night just 10 weeks previous. So, let me take you back to the 20th of March 2016.

It was a regular Sunday morning in a house with teenage kids. My daughter Casey had left to go to a friend's house, and I had made arrangements to pick her up that night at 11.20 from the cinema in Roscommon. At about 10.50 I dragged myself out of bed (I had a long day of cramps from a vomiting bug) to leave and make my way in to collect her. Abbey, my then 15-year-old and youngest daughter, was in her room listening to music. As I went down the stairs, she shouted after me, "Wait for me, I'm coming too.", and off we went together, listening to Celine Dion in the car on the way.

We were between banter and singing when we were stopped at the railway crossing in Ballymurray. "God, I hope she doesn't leave the cinema before I get there," I said to Abbey, as we waited for the train to pass. A couple of minutes later as we approached a part of the road on the Athlone side of Roscommon town where the large stone wall starts and the trees hangover, we saw a line of traffic. Then suddenly, with no indication or warning, a car pulled out and headed straight for us at high speed. His headlights went out. We had nowhere to go — BANG....

I woke up some days later in the Critical Care Unit in Tullamore Hospital where I had been placed in an induced coma to allow my body to rest. I had suffered catastrophic injuries, which included a broken neck, a fractured back, multiple broken ribs, and shattered femur and tibia which are now held together with a metal plate from my right hip to ankle, a fractured left knee, and a traumatic brain injury. Worst of all, I didn't know my daughter, Casey, at all and I had no recollection of other family members. Casey later informed me that the only words I uttered and kept repeating were, "I'm never too far away," as she and my father sat at my bedside.

My hospital stay is a very vague memory. My first recollection of being there was a priest praying over me with several voices in the background which sounded like a scrambled radio station. This was in the first couple of weeks after the collision. My next was Advanced Paramedic, Brendan Clerkin, who came to my bedside and introduced himself to me and told me he wanted to see how I was doing. Brendan was the paramedic who travelled with me from the crash scene to the hospital. I still didn't know at this point why I was there or what had happened. I remember Brendan walking away that day as if it were only yesterday. This was my first real memory of conversation. My mind was so confused, I wanted him to come back but I couldn't call him. Nothing would come out, just tears with no sound. I remember trying to focus my eyes on him as he walked away. With double vision, I could see three people over to the right, a tv screen, and metal bars. *'Where am I and why am I here?'* PANIC!

Abbey was upstairs in the pediatric ward waiting on surgery to repair her shattered wrist and to have wires in to help it knit. It turned out she also had contusions of both lungs and being an asthmatic, she couldn't go under anesthesia until her breathing stabilized, which thankfully it did. The gentleman who crashed into us, having had severe unresolved mental illness, passed away. The whole situation was a disaster.

A few weeks later Abbey and I left the hospital and went to my parent's house to rehabilitate. This was a welcome decision at the time as I was bedridden and needed regular medication. I needed

24-hour care. I had regained memories of family and felt being at my parents' house would be the best place to recover as my parents had not long completed an extension, which included a downstairs bedroom and wet room, which would be more suitable on our journey to recovery. Gardai arrived within a few days of us leaving the hospital and they took statements. A living nightmare had begun.

Picture this; I was stuck to a bed, one leg up and braced, the other down, and both arms out and squared in position because my muscles were so badly damaged. I had a Miami J collar on my neck and several broken ribs while having over two hundred stitches. Abbey shared the room with me but our conversation about the crash was very minimal. Hurt, angry, and fit to kill would be a total understatement as to how I felt for what the driver had put my kids through. Why us?

Abbey's night terrors had started, she would wake screaming in her sleep. She was hesitant to share her nightmares with me in case she would upset me. I had no idea how Casey was, because she stayed with a friend of mine outside Roscommon to study for her junior certificate at school and I had no memory of her early on. She had been visiting me with various family members whom I recognized, and while I was in hospital she had been sending me text messages daily, updating me on her days and telling me that she loved me, sending me pictures of a teddy that I had given her when she was only 7 years old, etc. It was only when I got my phone back and I was able to read these messages from her that I started getting my memory of her back, which thankfully, I did.

The time passed slowly as I tried to adjust to a new normal. It was an hour-to-hour, sometimes moment-to-moment struggle. I had to depend on my immediate family for basic care, such as showering and using toilet facilities, as there was no home care available. There was no follow-up by any mental health care agencies, leaving me with a feeling of complete isolation after such a traumatic event. I had to completely rely on my GP and family. I had such an over awareness of body sensations. I couldn't tell the difference between what was physical and what was emotional. I remember trying to maneuver myself partially onto my right side; it was like every bit of blood and fluid moved all at once on that side and the same happened in the other direction. I had no idea what was happening inside of my body. I struggled so much to identify with everything. That horrible feeling as I looked at all my wounds and the discoloration of my skin. Parts had no feeling at all. I wanted to vomit from the fear of my own body. As you can imagine my movements were very restricted, having a wash down in bed was a daily routine. A shower was out of the question at first because of the neck collar and the other wounds. My aim at this point was simply to get back to my own home and reunite with my kids, no matter what the consequences were.

I am tenacious by nature and my resilience is strong, so I knew I could do it, even if it could be difficult, but to top it all off, my long-term partner decided it was time for him to exit our relationship. This was the icing on the cake, everything that I was once accustomed to was now gone. I was broken in every sense of the word both mentally and physically. However, even though I was aware that my life would be completely different to what it had been, I did not want to be a victim of my circumstances, because I knew it was going to end with a very bad outcome.

I hovered between '*Why did I survive this?*' to '*Why didn't God take me? I am no good to my kids anymore. I can't do this, it's too painful. I don't want to be here anymore.*' Everything had changed, and I was in the greatest battle of my life, my mind being my greatest opponent. I knew that if I was to survive. I had to take control of my life or circumstance and defeatism would. I had to take back my power and make some major decisions. That day I made three decisions.

The first was that within one week I would move back to my own home, regardless of injuries and my lack of mobility survival skills. At least I could be with both my girls. My eldest daughter, Savannah, lived only 20 minutes from Roscommon, and I hadn't seen my granddaughter in some time so being close would make it easier. The second decision was that I would come off pain medication. My body sensations and signals were compromised, and I felt I needed as little interference as possible going forward, if I were to regain a level of normality. I needed to connect with my body again. The third decision was that I would drive my car again. I knew that if I didn't do it early on, I never would. I had to take back my power. And so, I asked my father to take me out to my routine GP visit to get pain relief and a vitamin B12 shot. At the appointment I told Dr Conor Lynam that it would be my last day taking pain medication. He strongly advised against my decision, but I had made my mind up. I was coming off it and that was that.

When I was finished with Dr Lynam I was wheeled back to the car and as soon as we sat in, I told my dad that I wanted to drive to where the crash happened. His reply was, "Christ. Maeve! You can't. Would you take a look at yourself, this is crazy." I could see where he was coming from, but I made it clear that either I drive, or he gets a taxi home. I was determined, "The car is automatic, please, I can do this, I know I can. I have to do this, or I will never drive again." How I did it, I will never know. I felt numb but so focused on my right leg and foot as I gently accelerated. My arms and shoulders were so weak. My neck was still in its brace. My father said, "Maeve, what if we are pulled over by the gardai?" My reply was simply, "I have nothing left to lose." God, I will never forget the look of dismay on his face. Poor Dad.

I pulled in at the wall after the 20-minute journey out the Roscommon Road, pondered, and then called the gentleman in question every conceivable name you could imagine, *'What were you thinking?...Why did you do this to my kids?... Selfish bastard!... I hate you!... You thought you'd take me out, well, think again... If it's the last thing I do, I'll beat these injuries and I will protect my kids.'* I was furious.

I allowed what I know now to be my emotions to vent and then asked my dad to lift me into the passenger seat to drive me home. I now had a visual of the wall to match the picture of what was left of my car. I accomplished something big that afternoon. My determination from that moment on never ceased. I am certainly not saying it was easy, but embracing the power of decision, as broken as I was, allowed me to move from a feeling of being helpless to one of being hopeful and determined.

The following morning, I woke after only a couple of hours of broken sleep, which now had become my normal sleep pattern. My parents had come into the bedroom to see what Abbey and I would like for breakfast. I asked my dad to put everything in a black bag and told him that we were going home. I knew if I stayed there much longer, I was going to get sick. I called Casey to tell her that we would all be together again for the first time in months. The excitement and fear were overwhelming, but Casey and Abbey would be back in their own beds. They would have each other again. We had all missed Casey so much.

Going back home brought a sense of freedom and familiarity. I remember being wheeled from the car into the hall and hearing my voice echo as I spoke to Abbey. The sound of emptiness was strange. No sooner was I there than a thought ran through my mind, '*Shit, now what? I am the adult here and my kids need me.*' I wanted a miracle to happen. My faith, which I felt was quite strong over the years, was really going to be put to the test now, but honestly, I felt like I had enough tests and couldn't take much more.

That night, as I lay in my own bed, I had a full awareness of every sensation in my body, one that I hadn't identified with. '*What is happening to me?*' I tried to ignore all my fear, but I was completely rattled when I heard Casey scream for help in her sleep, followed by Abbey screaming my name. I couldn't get up to comfort them. At this point all I could do was listen to my kids whimper. It was heart wrenching. In desperation, my immediate thought was divine intervention, '*Jesus, please help me. Mother Mary from one mother to another please help my kids, Ease this pain. I can't do this. I don't even know who I am. I can't get up, please help me.*' My faith was always strong, I believed that I had come from a divine source and energy, some call it God, and if this source created me then it could certainly recreate me, and hopefully help me in the toughest times.

It was a very long night with roughly 3 hours sleep and what I would call a useless description of a living hell on earth; listening to intermittent screams for help. I felt useless and worthless, pathetic at the very least. What kind of a parent was I? I needed to use the bathroom, but my father wasn't there, and I certainly wouldn't call my kids. I could only imagine how mentally and emotionally exhausted they both were already. I had to get my head together — fast. I looked down at my legs and thought. *'You will do as I say.'* Then I looked at both my arms. They were black and badly swollen with the muscles hanging just above the elbow on each side. I could hear the doctor's voice in my head saying, "You have a displaced fracture of the C7 vertebrae in your neck, you must keep the collar on." I was completely torn between what I was told I could do and what I believed I could do.

The commode was not far from the bed, and I knew if I could slide my butt to the edge of the mattress, I could reach it. One step is all I would need to sit down. Determined, I did It. *'Yay me!'* Then I heard Abbey shout. "Mam, what are you doing?!" She started to cry, "Why didn't you call us?" At that very moment, another major decision was made. I refused to fail my kids. They didn't ask for this. I am supposed to care for them, not the other way around. Honestly, I didn't know *how* I would do it or what our new life would be, but my faith and hope helped me to at least be open to "I can do it" and that it would be okay, if I put my mind to it. I needed to see what could be, not just what was. I knew that my thoughts alone were not going to be enough to help me navigate a new life, my feelings would also have to correspond. But as I said, I had no clue at this stage what was physical and what was emotional. I no longer understood my body due to vagus nerve disruption (the largest nerve in the body also known as the wandering nerve) and a misfiring nervous system, yet I knew I had to trust the process and stick with it, if something positive was going to come from this.

I have since come to learn that trust is a huge part of taking your power back. I knew in my heart that if I was going to do this right, I not only had to change my thinking process and how I spoke to myself, but I also had to change how I spoke to others regarding my injuries and how I felt about the collision. I had to think well and feel well. No complaining or I would end up going back into past thought forms while knowing that with every thought comes an emotion, I had to completely trust this process. Trust isn't always an easy thing to do, especially when circumstances are difficult and you feel vulnerable, but I have learned that when you go through difficult times and you need to triumph over them, you must trust and let go of trying to get and do everything right. You need to trust that it will be okay, even if you haven't certainty, and most importantly you need to trust yourself, even if sometimes you don't think you have what it takes.

As kids, we grow to learn to put our trust in the people around us, which is all good and well, however when it comes to overcoming personal challenges, you have to trust yourself too. Think about it, we've survived one hundred percent of your worst days so far, so we have the strength and ability. I had to focus forward one bit at a time. I didn't have one hundred percent certainty that everything would be the way I wanted in the future, but I trusted that I would give it my best effort to make it better at least.

I decided to start with a visualization of me walking in my sitting room, I had to mentally see it and feel the excitement of these first steps. My mental attitude had to be strong, and my emotional resilience had to be at the forefront, if things were to improve. I had to connect with what could be and feel what it would be like to be well again, even if it was just in my mind to start with. It gave me a focus, something separate and different to the physical pain and limitations I had been experiencing. Visualizing was a start.

Now up to this point, I hadn't really thought much about the fact that I had sustained a brain injury in the crash but as I started to mentally and emotionally become stronger, it posed a bit of a challenge. As I started to get more mobility back, I noticed that I was having difficulty with my balance. My first initial response to this was, 'Aw, it has to be the plate in my leg that is causing the problem,' so I ignored it. I was on a mission to get better. But then I noticed a significant visual disturbance with light changes. For example, when it started to get dark in the evening or when I turned on the lights in the house, I would get blurred vision. At this time, my recovery involved attending several hospital appointments which brought me between Tullamore, Dublin, and Galway. I noticed while enroute to these appointments that my eyes were going fuzzy, the traffic coming towards me, and the colours of the cars were bothersome. This became very challenging late in the evening as the drivers put their headlights on. The brain injury never came into play in my mind as such. I just felt pretty messed up. I remember one night as I lay in bed hearing a whistle sound in my ears, it nearly drove me crazy. I asked my daughters if they could hear it, but they couldn't. Eventually, after a long search, the sound brought me down to the kitchen which was downstairs and to the back of the house. There was the tiniest hole at the back of a pipe under the kitchen sink. *'My God what is going on with me? How could I hear this from such a distance? There is something wrong with me.'*

Not long after this happened my children asked me to go for dinner with them. I wanted to do this for them. It was the least I could do. I remember having to talk to myself for days prior to that evening for fear of losing my balance and falling. I sat in the restaurant counting the minutes so that I could leave and go home but as more people arrived the sound of voices and cutlery clanging sent me into a state of panic and the visual disturbance arrived again as the evening started to darken. It was a setback. The panic to get outside was dreadful. The words, *'Please help me!'* screaming in my head, but once again I didn't want anyone to know that I was struggling and crying inside. When I did get outside and my vision normalized, I took a big deep breath, *'Focus Maeve, you've got this.'* Affirming my strength allowed me to calm myself and get back my focus.

63

There were many times like this over the following months that I was aware my brain wasn't playing ball, but I was determined not to give up, even though at times I really felt like it. It was like a tug-a-war between my brain and my mind sometimes, but with time I began to realize that accepting my brain wasn't the same and choosing to work with it not against it, helped me more than struggling. I learned that when you are faced with a challenge that's not within your control, fighting it and trying to change something you can't doesn't help, it just deflates your energy. "Managing" the situation and steering it in a new direction, however, is much more empowering. I couldn't change the fact that my brain was injured, even if I wanted to, but I sure as hell wasn't going to let it ruin my life. I had to learn to adapt so I could keep my focus and strength. A decision to make an appointment with an eye specialist was truly what I needed, so I did and found that I had to wear Irlen lenses to help with light adjustments. This meant that I wore sunglasses in hail rain or snow. I also remember a particular comment as I left my local post office, who the hell does she think she is one of the Kardashians?

I also couldn't change that my vagus nerve was damaged. The vagus nerve plays a key function to crucial parts of the body, such as controlling the heart rate and the digestive system. It is also responsible for the immune system. I knew nothing about the vagus nerve until after the crash when I presented myself into my doctor's office with an array of symptoms. After I ate my heart rate was very high followed by no balance until my food was digested. A fizzy drink was a no-no as it left me with an irregular heart rhythm and near fainting episodes. If I ate late in the evening, I would wake with my heart beating so fast that I would have to vomit and empty my tummy to get my nervous system to relax. It took me a long time to try and control all the symptoms. It meant a strict diet and no fizzy drinks at all. I could not allow myself to get hungry or to have an empty tummy as it brought on indigestion, again leading me to near faints and weakness.

So, as you can see, it was very much a case of trying to get my life back, whilst having a broken body and a brain and nervous system that did their own thing, but I had made a decision and was determined to take back my power and recover for me and my kids, with the aim of having a life we could enjoy. I knew it might not be easy, but I decided I would take control in any way I could, no matter how small my decisions and actions were to be. I jotted down what and how I felt after particular foods, for example, and I quickly learned that eating small amounts every two hours was a key part in keeping my balance and near faints at bay. No food after 6pm and drinking only water was the key to staying relaxed. With this information, I had more power to create a way forward. Instead of fighting and feeling bad, I looked at how I could make things as easy as possible for me to tap into my strength. Every decision, even the tiny ones, helped me to gain power over my circumstances so I could take ownership of my life. I got up every morning and put my makeup on, regardless of how I was feeling inside. Being strong was my only option for recovery. There was no way that I was allowing the crash or my injuries and scars to define me or defeat me. I also had to acknowledge that the crash was not my fault, but my healing was my responsibility.

When you're faced with a challenge, and you feel like it's a continuous uphill struggle it's really important to take ownership of your decisions and actions in every way you can. It's emotional self-regulation if you like. You can fully acknowledge and respect all the bad feelings you feel, but do not let them become you or own you. The only way you can move forward in any challenge is to take ownership of your life and focus on being a victor, not a victim.

Every morning, I set aside 45 minutes for myself before getting out of bed and then again in the late evening, where I would bring myself into complete relaxation. I decided to self-regulate my emotional state by putting myself into a future event instead of looking back. Now, I want you to think strongly about this because this is the wake-up call that I needed. We wake every morning, and our mind goes to something that we are already familiar with, whether that is a past event or something our mind is telling us will happen. Every thought gives an emotional feeling, so if you have a past event that has brought you hurt, well, your day is already determined for you by negative emotions. I'm sure you have often heard someone say that they got out of bed the wrong side and they weren't in the best of form. Well, I'd put money on it that their first thought was a negative one. So, I decided to quieten my mind while putting my hand on my heart and visualized myself fully healed. I would hear people telling me how amazing I looked and how well I had healed. I felt the happiness and gratitude attached to that each morning. I was in pain, but I would certainly master a positive thought that made me feel love in my heart. I became fully aware of my thoughts and if a very negative one came in, which it did, I would say *'Okay, I see why you are popping up but you're telling me a lie I know I can do this.',* and then I would see a cancel sticker and put it over that thought. This took practice and it had to be habitual, intentional, and very clear. The body's ability to heal is far greater than we can ever give it credit for, as is the mind's.

I'm here to tell you that you can do whatever you put your mind to. If I can do this, so can you. I have learned that nothing changes for you mentally, physically, or emotionally unless you change your thinking, a change in how you see things. You must *want* this, and you must literally make a conscious decision to get over yourself, even if sometimes your old thinking might fight against it. We attract what we think about in our mind and body most, and become accustomed to it over years, and when you decide to change, your mind and body will automatically say, *'Come on, get up, get that cup of coffee and do what you have always done in the mornings, forget meditating take it easy you are broken.'* But this is when you have to say to yourself: *'No, it's time to stay and listen.'* Your body may

67

retaliate to your command, and I certainly had several weak moments, but my commitment to heal and to be a parent was far greater than the negative thoughts that would frequent my mind. I remember looking in the bathroom mirror one morning and said, *'I don't particularly like you or know who you are, but you are going to do everything I tell you to do from here on out.'* I had to commit to recovery and get disciplined about it. Within weeks of my decision to overcome negative thinking I started to see changes. I had absolutely no tolerance for bullshit or for listening to comments like "You can't do that."

I started small and worked up from there. With a tin of peas in each hand, I slowly gave my muscles a taste of heaviness, so I could rebuild them. I went from that to weight-bearing on my legs by walking three steps for three days, then four steps for four days, and so on. I distinctly remember the morning that I walked eight steps with the tins of peas in hand, tears flowing but with no emotion attached. I even asked my daughter if I was crying and she replied, "Mam only you can know that." Another setback, my foot was beginning to droop or flop as I walked, my foot felt different and had discoloration across the top of it, but I kept on going until it started to feel numb. A trip to Dr Connor and a referral for an MRI scan showed a metatarsal fracture from the stress of walking on a weak bone. Back into a boot again for another 6 weeks. This happened twice within 12 months.

My general practitioner, Dr Conor Lynam, had strongly advised me that a referral to *Acquired Brain Injury Ireland* would be very beneficial to help in my recovery, but I was having none of it as I did not want to accept the fact that I had a brain injury, yet knowing that at some stage I had to accept it, if I was to fully recover. In my mind, it wasn't visible, so it was okay to ignore it. Nothing like clean hair and a bit of makeup to camouflage what was hidden behind the smile. Nobody ever really did see beyond the public facade, which did a great job preserving my inner despair. But on reflection I knew this was something I had to take ownership of, if I were to recover fully, I had to embrace everything, no matter how hard, and find out how I could best navigate my recovery given my situation. I was not going to let anything beat me, no matter how tough it was.

I took to doing research on how to heal the brain, which led me to Dr Corinne Allen in California, an international researcher who spoke about the importance of water and the brain. After listening to Dr Corinne speak, I decided to buy a Kangen water machine and I slowly accustomed my body to a pH level of 8.5, before eventually staying steady at 9.5. level. This helped me to reduce the acid levels in my body and minimize the near faint. I continued my research and soon stumbled upon another doctor, Dr Rhonda Patrick. Rhonda spoke about superfoods and their health benefits. This led me to the benefits of broccoli sprouts and beetroot juice. Researching and educating myself gave me a sense of control and it gave me options, and with each option came new possibilities for more empowering decisions. Little by little my mind started to play ball and get on my side, and day-by-day my body did the same. It took time but I connected to the power of decision.

So, as I press the fast forward button to this present moment. I can now look back and say, damn, you did a great job. It was probably the worst and best part of my life as I took on a journey of self-discovery. I would often say my circle is small but in honesty I don't even have a straight line. I don't let too many people in, I protect my energy and what I have built inside myself. I also decided last year that I would attend an EMT course with Medical Ambulance Service to see the healing of my body on a different level and also to understand and know the functions of the body and how it works. I found the theory side of this course very beneficial, however it did trigger a post-traumatic stress response which I found challenging, so I left just weeks before the completion date. I was quite happy to have also completed a First Aid Responder course and to be part of the Athlone Emergency Defibrillator group. On the bright side of this I know a little more when it comes to helping others in times of need. I know firsthand what this feels like, and I will always be eternally grateful for the National Ambulance service and their quick response and also for the decisions Brendan made on that dreaded night.

Last November, after all this time, I decided to get in contact with Acquired Brain Injury Ireland. I now have a weekly meeting with Dr

Brian McClean (Clinical Psychologist) who has given me the ability to see myself through a different lens and also to find the parts of Maeve that are still here. This I am so truly grateful for.

This week I took a trip with my family to the promenade in Galway. I stood and observed the hundreds of bodies as they lay soaking up the sun in order to get that beautiful, bronzed look. Yes, that was me not so many years ago. This time around I stood, took a deep breath in, and affirmed '*I am one with all of this beauty. I am so grateful to be alive. I am so grateful for my daughters, my grandchildren, and my family.*' I felt the love in my heart so deeply as I affirmed those words. I could feel a lump in my throat as I clenched my teeth and the muscles of my jaw together and thought of her, the Maeve that used to be. Damn, I do miss her sometimes. As I looked out across the bay and embraced the beautiful smell of the fresh sea air and admired the different shades of blue that lay ahead of me, I realized that I was so truly in love with so many memories of my past and that this too was okay. I am okay. I knew at that very moment that I was showing vulnerability but instead of saying. '*Oh shut up, get a grip, and get over yourself.*' I did the opposite, I HELD ME.

I now see beauty in everything. I know that love conquers all. Life is a projection of oneness, or should I say the relationship and its strength between our thoughts and our emotions that emerge as one. As you think so you shall be. There is no such thing as failure,

71

the word only reflects the fact that you have tried and that you must get up and try again. In this life we will come to many crossroads, each road leads to a new destination and each with a new experience. Listen carefully to the voice within, the one that is deep in the pit of your tummy. The voice in the head is not always correct, remember to hit that cancel button. Love with intensity, feel it, embrace it, keep your thoughts in the present, and look only to the future. The universe will respond. IT HAS YOUR BACK.

Acknowledgements

I wish to acknowledge with heartfelt gratitude:

Mr. Brendan Clerkin Advanced Paramedic, NAS.

Mr. Barry Flynn Paramedic, NAS.

Dr Thomas Baer, Consultant Orthopedic Surgeon, Midlands Regional Hospital Tullamore Co Offaly.

Dr Murphy, Midlands Regional Hospital Tullamore.

Dr Conor Lynam and the staff at Newtown Medical Centre, Athlone.

Dr Brian McClean, Clinical Psychologist, Acquired Brain Injury Clinic.

Dr Joe Steiner. Steiner Chiropractic.

Deirdre, Pat, Adam, Simon, and Laura Leonard, Lecarrow, Co Roscommon

Garda Stephen McDonagh, Garda roads policing unit, Roscommon town.

Mr. Andre Sologub, Mullingar.

My immediate family and all those who helped during my recovery.

CHAPTER 4

This too, shall pass.

by Paula Esson

In my life I have learned that experiences and events are perpetually changing, revolving, swaying and swinging, our desire to control these pulsing metronomes often result in intense feelings of confusion or a lack of clear direction in our lives. I feel these moments are the start of something truly magical and are the very essence of our personal expansion.

"This too, shall pass" has become my security in life, life buoy, and my protection both mentally and physically. As the months and years have gone by the ebb and flow of stories which I will share through this chapter I have reached the gentle realization that the answers are in our ability to stay still in the eye of every storm and act in between the ticking of the clock. Those spaces where chaos cannot reign or even exist. Obstacles are gentle messages to help us create better decisions, slow down and protect ourselves.

The meaning comes from Persian poetry that neither the bad, nor good, moments in life ever indefinitely last. Everything is temporary. If we can adopt this mindset, it can be supremely empowering, granting permissions to slow the worrying about events we cannot control, to allow us to move through adversity with grace, knowing that whatever the situation, it will soon be behind you. Making this decision at the core of your life can lead to vastly less stress on your mind and body and super-boost your ability to create a brilliant foundation for your future. It is encouraging and reassuring. To quote Solomon's Seal "THIS ALSO SHALL PASS AWAY."

Knowing that whatever situation you find yourself in right now, it does not define the outcome, in fact it is the laying of the pathway for your future. Today, I cannot see my computer screen, my eyes cannot focus. Immediately I think my eyesight is deteriorating; the fact is I didn't slow down long enough in a client session to realize we had accidentally switched glasses. Now two of us can't see what we are doing and have eye strain for the next 7 days until we can meet!

This is the kind of event that tells my heart to slow down, sit down and check my environment before I make my next move. So many small actions piled on top of one another can lead to humorous happenings like this or grades of chaos that make for a bumpy road. This too shall pass... in 7 days.

The phrase "This too, shall pass" has allowed me to maintain a very positive outlook in the most extreme adversities and scenarios whilst holding my dignity and boundaries in the knowledge that most emotional interactions that feel impossibly tough are usually tears from their soul desperately trying to be seen or a set of odd circumstances that I could have prevented or steered, had a I "slowed down to smell the coffee" as such.

This is not to say that I have mastered this piece, far from it even as a neurologist and pain management specialist for three decades, however, I have reached a place where it is clear to me that if I stop and repeat the phrase "this too shall pass" I can regulate my nervous system, regain balance, prevent an outburst that I may later regret and harness a level of clarity that keeps me from teetering too far off track.

In my experience it is easy to succumb to these emotions and believe that the waves of situations and interactions and demand on our energy and resources will never end.

It's even more complex to witness these moments as wisdom and guidance. Quite the opposite, it can feel like you are drowning in a sea of human craziness where the next decision and choice you make is literally like playing an odd game of chess against the toughest games master in the room. your own mind. Professor Steve Peters created the superb book and model *The Chimp Paradox* ⑦ to help us all comprehend and make friends with your emotions and thoughts and understand how your mind is working at any point in time. Navigating the decision and choice process and slowing down to let yourself feel your way through is fundamental to success and can create a real vantage point and a proper frame of reference to feel and know if your next move is the right one for your life and your goals.

When I was 5 years old, in 1975, we lived in Rio de Janeiro, Brazil in an opulent apartment with servants, my world was one of beauty, laughter and love, parties and tropical food.

Forty feet away over the intricate metal balcony were the famous "Favelas", a warren of plastic bag sand corrugated roofs, breeze block walls notorious for crime, poverty and hardship woven into the notes of laughter, cooking, and football in the streets. The smells of steaming pots of seafood rice, Feijoada bean stews with fired fresh bread. The atmosphere was one of total contentment, activity, and fun amidst an extreme lack of resources.

My pure innocence and love as a child only saw the bright colours and excitement, kindness, and love. I never witnessed the suffering that lay underneath the wide smiles and the melodic Afro samba and Bossa nova music as it drifted towards the sky and filled every room and space either side of this human divide. I was often ushered away by the staff, who felt my impressionable mind would be filled with the "wrong messages", but nothing would keep me away from my tiny hands holding the cool bars of the balcony as I sat in a squat position for hours absorbing the happiness and the vibrance from below. The divide could not be clearer, I made many friends over the years and attribute my sporting ability to the time spent in the dirt of the back allies under the blistering sun, amidst the joy and character of the notorious "Favelas".

It was these 9 years that defined me and showed me the way, it was also to become my weakness and blind spot all the way into my late forties, the innocence leading to allowing other people take control of my decisions and ultimately my life's direction in adulthood, until I harnessed the awareness and vision to return to trusting my heart and literally my soul. It is these experiences over the years that have been gathered here to inspire you and allow you to truly trust your heart through careful action and reflection.

To give this context, I almost became a voyeur to my own life. The simplicity and motion in Brazil was in extreme contrast to the structure of life in the United Kingdom. There were multiple times where I genuinely could not see agendas, manipulation, unhealthy energy or situations that empowered others but left me without any control of the outcome.

It was 1997 and as a creative and a high drive to provide to my community, I used all my basketball skills to develop the first ever academy in Hexham Northumberland. We had 80 players from aged 8 through to 25. I was the first female coach to be leading a men's team. It was an age of progression, excitement, gender equality blasting through opinions, ideologies and the "Status Quo". My absolute dream role. I was to be blindsided though, the signs were there, I just chose to ignore them, keeping my simplicity in place and the goal of winning the league, and assisting players to reach the ultimate goal of playing for England.

A mature male coach had joined the squad without interview. Within the space of 5 months the map and strategy had changed and his influence as a doctor moved through the mindset like osmosis. I could feel it, the entire atmosphere changed, the warmth, friendship, family feel departed and was replaced by a "win at all costs" agenda, even in the under 8's squad. All my values were eroded, my naivety allowed this to happen. A number of key observations highlighted that there were a number of obvious flashpoints that I needed to understand.

I held people on pedestals. Just by their titles with no evidence. I wasn't able to stand strong in my position and I learnt that people almost smell this weakness and change allegiance. I really needed approval from people, and this led to wobbling and making poor decisions. I left myself vulnerable to unhelpful criticism and responded in unhelpful ways.

When I resigned, it was a knee jerk reaction, an emotive one. I was comparing my dream and my passion for the sport with the negativity I was experiencing. The fun was gone. Rather than making my strategy and plans super clear to all involved and leading through inspiration, I just left. This was a pattern that repeated at work as well. I learnt over 25 years to take some space and trust the process, that this too will pass and be steadfast and calm in my communications and attitude, and I stopped leaving every situation that felt uncomfortable and flipped it to a positive challenge instead, and an opportunity for growth as well as very firm evidence that the choppy seas were a sign of success and levelling up to the next platform and not a sign of failure or a straight request to bail out.

Stepping into the unknown is the most positive and life-affirming action you can take. If you have seen Indiana Jones and the Last Crusade, the "Leap of faith" defines a moment of pure triumph. The path is not clear, it genuinely appears to not exist. All Indie must do is step out into the unknown and trust he will be caught safely. Whilst being chased by his demons as such. With a deep, deep breath…. He launches and finds himself standing on solid ground, camouflaged as a deep ravine that would surely lead to his demise. He is safe, and if he has changed his perspective by 45°, the path was as clear as black and white.

We can only move forwards, we must let go to let life and health naturally reveal itself, what we need to be super clear on is what we are falling towards and into. This needs to be an upgrade defined by you and only you.

Trusting your Heart and Gut

How do you know you are making the right decision for your life? A decision that will propel you towards your heartfelt wants? How do you know what it feels like? Even more importantly, how do you know you are veering off piste and into the trees without navigation and soon to be so lost in the wrong behaviour and supremely awful decisions?

In 2015 I was about to be offered the opportunity of my life (or I certainly thought so). I had the enthusiasm and energy of a gazelle; the planets had aligned in my career to take on the position of Principal of a private training college for physical therapy. It was the pinnacle of my last 25 years of endeavors, I could now implement all my visions, creations, excitements, and plans and lead my team to unprecedented success in my field. I could see it now, witness it in my mind so clearly. There would be hundreds of students rushing to my door, teachers would follow my plan seamlessly and with zest, activity and enthusiasm, the dream of having established a footprint solidly, planted a flag clearly in the field of progress for pain relief.

Now let's fast forward these 3 years to 2018. The college was returned to its owner, I was a washed-out dishrag, in shock that, in my perception, it was the behaviour of others that dictated the outcome and squeezed me towards the decision to return it from whence it came. In calm hindsight and reflection, this genuinely wasn't the case at all. Let me explain.

81

The decision to engage in the company as a director was made with my rose-tinted glasses on, my heart was full of hope, pride, and dare I say, innocently blind ego. My history as a teacher with the college also meant that I was making decisions through a love for the work and sentimentality, my emotions were leading the way. I was already a company director of health centres, this wasn't a case of I couldn't make logical, sensible, planned, and well thought out decisions. The action was taken through love, love for the techniques that could potentially help people live comfortable lives, respect for the staff involved and pure purpose in relation to the advancement of pain management.

I learnt in hindsight that there are some very important and critical elements to decision making, especially when it involves your reputation, finances, time, family, and your health.

I was single-minded, dedicated to the purpose, resolute and firm. I had this! This was going to be great. I was batting off any negativity, any objections, observations, calm thoughtful facts, historical evidence, and the true voice of people I admired and trusted.

My pure desire for success was running through the process at warp speed, I didn't stop once to reflect, reverse, or conjure up any sensible joined up thinking. So, what had I omitted from this hugely important moment before I took a heartfelt deep breath, smiled, and picked up my 45-year-old fountain pen to etch my signature on the contracts. This is what I discovered.

Gut Instinct

I had a hunch, a dull, rumbling, nagging sensation that transcended any rational thoughts that involved "business", "paperwork" and systems. It just would not leave me alone; it pervaded every thought as the date came closer to signing. It whispered to me in the night...*something is wrong,* my brain was scanning every memory, event and activity related to the college that I had experienced already, and it was most certainly not coming up "Green for Go", pop the champagne, put your dancing shoes on. It was literally pulling me back by my shirt, metaphorically shaking its head in its hands, screaming at me to stop and breathe, take more time. In life terms I didn't do my due diligence. The problem was, I didn't listen, I wrapped those thoughts and very genuine feelings of doubt, resistance and "put on the brakes" and ignored it all. So consequently, I headed into a proverbial car crash in business and life.

These feelings are top of the pile when making decisions. Harvard University has recently confirmed that weighing both sides of a decision is key. Personally, I am extremely sensitive to my surrounding emotional and physical environment, and I know so many of us are this way too, it's just been forced out of us, downgraded, and put on the back burner in comparison to the power of hard facts and data. This can potentially be very disarming and lead us into some very unhelpful places. It is important though to differentiate gut instinct from fear. Are you able to define the two clearly within your own body and mind? Fear thrives in doubt and busyness whereas gut instinct is strongly linked to a whispering intuition about a scenario, and both need to be listened to closely.

Fear can also feel deeply uncomfortable physiologically, my favourite is to flee, evacuate, eject. The slightly less fun side effect of these responses means I do end up reading the Beano in the bathroom feeling that my body and brain really take this decision-making process way too seriously at times. Truth be known though; this is now my litmus paper when faced with making important life changing moves now. I call it "the closet" test.

The Closet Test

At first, I thought my body was my biggest enemy, it would show up with these untimely demands that needed some very inconvenient fast decisions. At first, I thought it was IBS (irritable bowel syndrome), it was irritated alright, annoyed I was about to take an action that would one dice move towards the slidey snake on the game board and spiraling down we would go. I learnt to listen to this more closely, then measured it against some of the life moves I was making in very recent years. It showed up around people in my life, business projects, certain environments. Acting like divining sticks looking for water! When I followed this directly, it navigated me away from situations that weren't mutually supportive, progressive, fair, productive, safe, or trusted. It took me 52 years to get there. Hopefully, this can save you from some unwanted scenarios in life.

It's not a dodgy curry always, it's a neurological response that you are about to march clear off the path.

The Rapid Test

The rapid test helps you not think more than three seconds and to feel your way quickly through. For example, I was in a bar in Borovets Bulgaria in 2023.

A group of rather "happy" young men on a stag do entered the bar...rather fell into the bar to be fair, while we were calmly watching snowboarding on TV and sipping the rather delicious local beer delivered in frosty iced glasses. The game that started was to somersault their friends backwards at speed and then celebrate if they landed on their feet. The next target was us. Some part of me thought this was a phenomenally silly decision, my friends concurred. I did the rapid test. I quite fancied the buzz...but it was dangerous potentially, being torpedoed headfirst into a concrete floor with broken glass on it. However, there was one sensible young man who was protecting the flying human's head and ensured safe landing. The men were all young and strong. Rapid test complete... I was next seen flying through the air and landing with style, safely. Would I do it again, never.

The rapid test is a quick yes / no tool. Write the scenario down on a piece of paper. For example, shall I take on this new job role? Write yes and no below it. Walk away for 4 hours and come back to circle your answer straight away. This really helps to make more measured and reasoned responses and stops any direct pressure as well from outside influences. If you are spontaneous like me, this can be helpful.

The Value Test

One of the areas that have gone supremely wrong when decision making in my life is becoming involved in projects and work commitments with people and companies where the values don't align. Relying on the "it will all be okay" approach generally can't keep the momentum flying when the deep beliefs are not aligned. For this situation, clarity on your own core values is key, a few of mine would be freedom, equality, inclusiveness, compassion, integrity, honesty, respect, and accountability. The most deeply aligned value in my world would be trust.

After a long day when you feel you have had a rough run, nothing is working in your direction, you feel unheard, not appreciated, and frazzled. Place the scenario that frustrates you most onto paper. Wait a few hours and write your value next to it and align the values of the scenario. If they don't match, decide to change the project or role or even delegate. For example, in 1998 I was coaching high level Basketball, at the time, very much a man's game. The male head coach had to depart in the middle of a tournament. The only one around to pick up the gauntlet was me. There was clearly an undercurrent of opinion amongst the players that I could not possibly take this role or lead them in strategy, strength, and passion. The first fifteen minutes were diabolical, not a single play was completed as planned, not one player listened to side-line input and strategy. What ensued was chaos.

My core values were being supremely challenged, I was hot, not thinking straight, and outright panicking. I was losing control of the game; the deep value was that I wasn't good enough as a woman to fill this role. This was etched all over my body language and I stopped in effect. To lead effectively and with strength. The squad sniffed that out in the air and continued to ignore the coaching. I was flustered, jabbering somewhat, and moved to screaming instructions whilst flapping my arms like a crazy person. At half time, and 43 points down, Sky TV were lamenting my coaching, being phenomenally sexist and had turned me into a laughingstock. The feelings were raw and real. Every sinew in my body wanted to run. I went to the bathroom and locked myself in. I wrote the problem on my whiteboard and the core values that were being challenged. I realized quickly that my deep values were shattered in this scenario. I really needed to walk away. Instead, I decided to write the core values they needed from me right here, right now. These were leadership, strength, boldness, commitment, and courage.

This is what I went back onto the court with. I took the reins and suddenly everyone fell into line, the captain backed me up telling everyone to "Be quiet! Listen to the coach!". I aligned with their values relating to what they needed, and we still lost by 5 points, but it was a brilliant performance with grit and commitment. By understanding their needs, I was able to install some of my values into them, respect, trust, accountability.

I went on to ensure that many more women became coaches of male teams from the under 11's all the way to senior. When making decisions, in this case, run or stay.

1) Work out which of your values are being crossed? Why does this upset you or lead you to unhelpful responses such as arguing or leaving?

2) What values do the other people have in the scenario? If you can't work them out. Ask.

3) Align with their values in your mind (not necessarily action, especially if it is around more hostile values).

4) Observe how they install the software of your values that you want activated and watch how the situation often leads to a result, happier atmospheres and everyone being heard. Usually leading to a positive outcome and success.

Everything is duality, the yin, and the yang, positive and negative. I chose to decide on only one side of the coin, what I wanted to see and what I wanted to happen in the future. My head was in a cloud of naïve adventure, mixed with the sense of anticipation and heady success.

In my mind If I was to use a knife, it would be to make an exotic, delicious, heartfelt meal, never to cause harm. Having this way of thinking is potentially problematic though, and can unbalance the decision-making journey, and create results that are not so robust. Being aware of all the potential dimensions of the decision is key.

Trusting my own power to make the right decision and take dynamic action has now been reduced to just a few factors on both sides of duality.

The Warmup List

They listen.

I feel respected and valued.

I have a "Lean in" feeling.

I get an excited and positive feeling inside.

Laughter and smiling.

The situation involves bringing skills together for mutual gain and a social or business service / upgrade for society.

Clear process, outlines, and structure.

I have clarity and vision. I can clearly see the pathway to results.

I'm buzzing and feel elevated in my life. A true uplift.

The Cool off List.

Do they value me?

Do I feel uneasy in the person's company? Want to lean away?

Do I feel tense? Can't find my flow of words.

Do I have a nagging drag in my stomach?

Do I feel safe?

Do I observe they are working out how to use my skills for their gain rather than a mutual collaboration. This is ultra-important to me.

Do I have a clear blueprint on how we are moving forwards?

Do I feel pushed and pulled to make decisions in an untimely manner?

Are they authentic?

Do they use psychological techniques to gain my commitment.

These can often be misunderstood as nervousness or fear around a new project. The experience is very different though if it is a mutual relationship.

When your intuition kicks in, follow your heart and gut instinct closely to open up your possibilities and when it whispers to you to reverse, or you don't know why you feel apprehensive, it is best to keep away from backward somersaults.

CHAPTER 5

Reflection And Giving Yourself Some Time

by Gerard Smith

Since birth, I have faced many challenges, personally and professionally. In this section of the book, I wish to share my experiences of overcoming all the challenges I have faced over the years, and possibly inspire you to overcome any challenges that you may be experiencing.

I was discovered to be deaf by my mother when I was a year old, when one day she noticed that I did not react to a doorbell when a visitor came to the house, particularly when the door was closed. She proceeded to get my hearing checked with an audiologist and the audiologist of the day was convinced that I was able to hear and did not require any hearing aids.

By the time I was 4 years of age, the audiologist informed my parents that they were not 100% sure if I was deaf either. As there was no audiology technology in the late seventies the audiologist at the time was not sure if I was deaf or not. Unsure what to do about my hearing, they decided to give me one hearing aid. In their opinion, I could be deaf in one ear and hearing in the other.

As technology improved, at 6 years of age they could confirm that I was in fact deaf in both ears and gave me my second hearing aid. However, I could not get used to wearing them both because I got the two hearing aids at different times, so I ended up wearing one hearing aid for most of my life.

I went to a deaf school from 1979 to 1993 in Dublin and went on to further education after my leaving certificate, including Post Leaving Course and IATI (accounting technician).

In 1996 I started to work for Mitsubishi Motors' main distributors on the Naas Road, Dublin. During my time there I developed a great working relationship with my colleague within the organization and with all the main dealers throughout the country. Most of the working relationship with the dealers was done by phone. Let me explain the level of deafness I have. As you are aware, deafness is a hidden disability, and no one knows if a person is deaf or not unless they go up to them to have a chat. I will use blindness as a demonstration here of the different levels of deafness. A completely blind person would need a long white stick, braille, and a guide dog to function, whereby a person who is slightly blind would use a pair of glasses from an optician to correct their vision. The same applies to deafness, I would use hearing aids to correct my hearing level.

During my early career I moved jobs, gained new experiences, and met new people. A lot of the work I did was either in person or over the phone. In January 2001, I started to work for a commercial vehicle dealership. I worked in the dealership as a service department receptionist and dealt with a lot of phone calls, booking vehicles in, updating clients regarding their vehicle, generating invoices, and providing cover for breakdown services by sending a mechanic out to repair the vehicle or arrange a tow truck to recover a vehicle to bring back to the dealership.

I was enjoying my service receptionist role until near the end of my three-month probationary period, when I was called into the service manager's office. The service manager informed me that he was letting me go, since he felt I was unable to use the phone correctly and told me that he was giving me 2 weeks' notice to leave my position. While it shocked me, I requested that he should put my dismal into writing, and he agreed. Later in the afternoon, I received the letter as promised from the service manager only to find that he did not write down exactly what he had said in our conversation, on paper he extended the 2 weeks' notice to 4 weeks.

In light of this, I used the full 4-week notice working for the company and with the support of my dad I found a new job which was also based in Dublin. During my time working to 4 weeks' notice in the old company I had faced many challenges, especially keeping my motivation to get up to go to work to deal with all the negative atmosphere within the office, which I felt was toward me. It was also difficult finding my replacement sitting at my desk when I arrived at work one morning. At that point when I met this replacement, I was not even sure if I had a new job. I had bought a house 9 months earlier, so it was a scary thought not to have a job.

My dad in particular was not one bit happy by the way I was treated within that workplace, and as my main supporter in the situation he encouraged me to look at the equality acts, that at the time were in infancy stage. He reached out to a government agency who would assess all cases to see if there were any breaches within the equality acts relating to my dismissal. Luckily for me I had kept all my notes outlining each incident that had happened within the 3 months of working in that employment. The department assessed my case and deemed that I had a reasonably good case to hold my previous employer accountable for their actions. I started in the new job in Dublin as soon as I completed my notice from the old job. For the first 13 months in my new employment, I had a court case hanging over me while I was being trained in a very responsible job. It was stressful. I worked with my solicitor from the Department of Equality to put the best case forward. This was done mainly over the phone.

I remember the day I was in court; there were three judges. One judge was for the employer, the second judge was for the employee, and the third judge was chairperson of the other two judges. This day was my most challenging day ever in my life. With my level of hearing, I had to concentrate greatly on what was going on and what was being said, and watching the body language between judges, my previous employers, and other people who were in the room, while the case was going on. What I noticed about the judges was that they spoke very low at a distance away from everyone and I had to concentrate in greater detail. It's how I wanted to prove to the judges that I was capable to have a conversation with anyone either face to face or on the phone.

In the courtroom, when the defendants and their barrister were asked questions, they were regularly asking the judges to repeat the questions as they were unable to hear the judges correctly. This went on for the whole day. The defendant brought in an independent witness, a contractor who looks after certain tasks that the company outsources, whereby he mentioned when questioned by the defendant barrister a scenario that I was talking to him about, regarding a truck having a headlight issue and when it arrived down to his workshop, he found that it is an indicator issue. This example provided by the witness allowed my solicitor to demonstrate and ask a question. First, she repeated the two words (headlight and indicator) a few times and then asked the question, "Can you identify that they are two different words while you were on the phone to my client?" The defendants and their legal team went into shock. Other witnesses attended on the day, and I felt that they did not make any impact on the case for both me and the defendant other than the contractor.

My solicitor made her closing statement that she had only met me three times during the whole process, twice at the start of the process and on the day of the court. All communications were done over the phone no matter what environment I was in. At one stage she rang me while I was on the bus travelling home from work to ask a question.

The outcome of the court case was in my favour. In 2003, I decided to go back to college and get myself a degree. I studied an honours Bachelor of Arts degree in Management and Information Systems, which is managing a company or running a business through IT. I did this course as an evening course while working during the day.

During my time in this education period, I had to deal with large numbers of people in the classroom. Bear in mind I was used to being in a small class of 7 to 9 students when I was in school. That said, being in college meant I was fortunate enough to work alongside other students who also assisted me to overcome certain bits in the class that I may have missed. Also, the lecturers, once they knew that I had some form of deafness, made themselves available to answer any questions I may have had. We shared notes between us and sometimes if they didn't understand a particular topic in the subject, we figured things out between us.

From the time of starting to work in the large organisation in Dublin, I had the aspiration to work to the top of the company and started applying for various promotions as soon as I could. At my early part of working in this company, they did not provide any interview feedback, which I started to take up and the HR department decided to implement this for all interviewees. This was fine until the last interview I had with the company. This is my most memorable interview.

It was a summer day, and the interview room was hot, although the window was open. There were 3 interviewers interviewing me for the position in the Chief Engineer Department where I would manage and supervise the staff who were doing the same role I was doing. During the interview process, the middle interviewer proceeded to ask me a question. As he started asking the question a very loud noise from a bus was going past the window, and the interviewers could not hear what being said. One of them went to the window to close it. The middle interviewer knew my capability to lip read and to overcome any interruptions that may come into place. The person who went to the window closed it just as the middle interviewer finished his question and I started to answer his question. At the end of this interview, I felt great leaving the room having displayed my capabilities to overcome any obstacles and answered all the questions correctly due to my experience.

The company in question encouraged people who were unsuccessful in getting their promotions to go for interview feedback. I had used this service a couple of times prior to this interview. The HR specialists who happened to be in the interview provided the interview feedback. During our conversation he mentioned that I was "stupid" at the interview. and that I did not qualify for the promotion. I left the room feeling very confused and shocked. It knocked my confidence and I questioned and doubted myself for a number of months afterwards.

Later that year, I met a guy who was heavily involved in a political party as a volunteer. He knew I was a deaf person. During this time there was a campaign within the deaf community to get Irish Sign Language recognised as a third language in Ireland. He was also aware of this, due to the fact that he had a distant relation who also happened to be deaf, and he was following this himself. He encouraged me to join this political party and to see if we could get the Irish sign language recognised from within a political party. I decided to join this political party as I could contribute toward something that would be very beneficial for the deaf community in Ireland.

In the process of my Sign Language proposal to the political party annual general meeting I paid a visit to a charity organisation that looks after the deaf community; for people who develop hearing loss later in life, and people who suffer from tinnitus. During my meeting with the CEO of the organisation, he asked me if I liked going to meetings, which I answered yes. He then asked me if I was interested in joining the board of directors for this charity organisation and in March 2013, I joined the board of directors.

For next couple of months while I was settling myself in as a director of an organisation, I realised that what had been said at my recent interview feedback in my place of employment was unfounded by me.

During the early part of my career as a director of an organisation, I also realised the responsibility that comes with making a good contribution to ensure that an organisation is functioning at its fullest potential. The decision to be part of a board of an organisation affects the lives of the staff and the client who are receiving the service from the organisation. Over a number of years, I grew more confident in myself as a board member and in 2016 I decided to create a business.

I decided to create a company that would allow me to have my freedom, where I would not be under any obligation of working under a boss. Some people that suffer with disabilities will only limit themselves to what they are capable of doing but when it comes to my own mind, I see challenges that can easily be overcome, whether that be for business or personally. I created a translation company. I was still working in the organisation at the time and as with any new business, there were a few challenges in my new business, getting clients being one of them. I went to an event which entailed a presentation to promote all experiences that deaf people encounter on a day-to-day basis, in order to make the government aware of the of difficulties that deaf people have. While I was at this event, I discovered a major weakness in my business model, and based on that weakness I knew I could not prevent or protect my business from any negative actions that were out of my control. The business was not financially viable, so I closed it. Shortly after, I chose to create another business but unfortunately that did not work out the way I would have liked it to either, so I closed it too. However, despite the two businesses not working out, I was determined to create a successful business.

In early 2019 I went to a networking event in Dublin where I met a lovely gentleman called Brian. Brian introduced me to a technology that recycles plastics into biofuel and invited me to join him to create a company called Passionate About Recycling (PAR). This was another stab at running a business other than the charity.

Brian and I have one thing in common. We were both deaf. As you are aware about me, I am deaf from birth whereas Brian became deaf later in life. He is known within the charity as a person who has an acquired hearing loss. By being in business with Brian, and other directors of this company, I learned a lot about the sales process and how to go about generated business. I never considered myself as a salesperson but from the lessons I learned from Brian, I was able to bring one of the largest recycling companies to the table as a client and that was an achievement in itself.

Then, in 2020, Covid-19 happened, and I took time out to really sit down and think about things. I thought about what I had done in the past, where I was currently, and where I would like to go in the future. Looking back, my interests in business started when I was in school. My class was in charge of running a coffee shop where we were responsible for everything between buying stock, creating profit, and earning a percentage of the profit. I found the way of doing business and how it works very exciting and intriguing. I worked in this until I left school.

I also joined a sign language organisation which was destined to closure as a treasurer. I turned the organisation from a loss making to a very profitable one within 18 months by encouraging other members of the board to play their part in getting new clients through the door. I also joined a golfing society which was struggling financially as a treasurer. I managed to ensure that there was a small profit generated by the time I became a captain of the society. With all the planning for the year including my captain day, the society generated a nice profit for 2013 year, and I had 37 guests at the captain day which was not the record. It was the highest attendance for a number of years. Golfing Societies were on a decline due to the golf clubs were getting very competitive with their membership fees.

101

Reflecting on my past and present opened my eyes to many things, and I decided to create another company while working alongside PAR. I decided to become a property investor so I could diversify my income from PAR and other organisations. I took up a property investment training course and learned all the various nuances of mitigating property risks in 2020. Since my training course, I invested in properties in the UK, Ireland and Spain.

In 2022, I felt I had the confidence to go out on my own. I chose to leave the organisation I had been working with for 21 years to go and achieve my goals in life. I reached out to an old work colleague, Martin, to let him know that I had handed my notice into my place of employment. He had left the company in 2019, so we met for coffee, and he updated m me on what he had been doing since. Following that meeting he introduced me to his cousin Chris, who was spearheading the business. Since then, I have been working alongside Chris, Martin, and their team, for which I am now part of. We are on an exciting journey with the new start up.

Brian and Martin were two positive people in my network, and they were very helpful when it came to removing any negative mindset I had. I also identified other likeminded people by attending networking events, people who you can do business with to ensure that you are successful in what you are doing and ensuring you have a positive mindset going forward.

Having the right people around you is so important as you grow in life and business. It gives clarity and allows you to focus on what you really want, and it allows you to achieve your goals with enthusiasm and passion. If you don't feel that your current network can assist you, join a networking event and you may find someone who can assist you after turning up on a regular basis. Allowing the right people to know your goals and being true to yourself can be very uplifting both personally and of course professionally.

Every day people make decisions that determine the direction of their lives. In my experience the best decisions are made when you take time out to reflect on life and its direction and the people that will accompany you on your journey. Without that reflective pause it's easy for decisions to be haphazard and random, and for decisions to be made for you that result in outcomes that aren't what you truly want.

Looking back at the most pivotal points in my life I can see that those were the times when I got clear about my outcome and made decisions to support them. Essentially, I took ownership, even if it meant making difficult decisions in challenging situations.
I would like to leave you with a few questions, in the hope they will inspire you to live your dreams.

1. What are your dreams?
2. How can I achieve my dreams?

3. How many steps do I need to take to achieve my dreams?
4. Who do I have in my network that can assist me to achieve my dreams?
5. Always have a positive attitude.

"I can achieve a lot! I can do a lot.

I can do all I set my mind to, all I can think of.

I have the self-esteem, the wisdom, the talents, the abilities.

I have the self-control, the boldness, the readiness.

I am ready to live my life.

I am ready to do things, be things and succeed.

I am ready for life:

YES, I am ready.

YES, I can.

CHAPTER 6

We will survive!

by *Heather Mortimer*

Friday 5th March 1999 was the day I gave birth to my second, beautiful son Liam — a fast and furious delivery, born 10 days early. Big excited brother Nathan was 26 months-old at the time and after nursery went straight to my parents. I loved being a mum and was so looking forward to being a mum again, but that day I made a huge decision. It was a decision that may come as a surprise to you considering the day it was, and I certainly did not envisage making it. I took off my wedding ring and chose to end my marriage.

My marriage had been great for many years, so ending it was not a flippant decision. I had considered all the pros and cons for the previous few months. I knew it would not be an easy road after the decision was made. It could mean I may have to support my children on my own, but living in a marriage without reciprocation of loyalty was not something I could do.

I was in my last year of a floristry course, believing that someday I would open a florist shop. At that moment in time, I was running a successful market stall selling hosiery, so aside from the hustle the most important weekend was ahead of me, ironically, Mother's Day. I had a lightbulb moment as I lay in hospital. If I were to pave a way forward for my children and me, I would have to create a financial foundation that would allow me to provide for them, alone if I had to. I knew that if I sold enough flowers that weekend, we would be okay for a few months. I wrote out my flower order on a scrap of paper in the hospital bed and called the wholesalers. Instead of my usual order I placed a much bigger one. It was a lot of money and a big gamble as I also needed good weather. However, I had a great power team of friends and family to help me out and make it a success. "The show goes on", as my dad would say, and I knew that if I focussed on work and on making it work, I would not break.

Getting ready to leave the hospital with my newborn. Liam, my mum and dad turned up with an excited big brother, Nathan, to take us home. Walking out into that cold corridor I remember saying to myself *'This is the first walk as a unit of me and my boys.'* Nathan was holding one hand and Liam was being carried in his car seat. I made a secret promise to myself, *'WE WILL SURVIVE'*, no matter what is thrown at us.

My ex-husband left the family home in September and made no contribution to me or the boys from that day. My parents had an amazing marriage — true respect, and love for each other for over 46 years of marriage. I had never heard an angry word between them. In a way, I felt I had let them down by choosing to bring up my children as a single mother.

On the route home, Mum was driving with Dad sitting beside her, and me and my two boys in the back seat. Mum said, "Why don't you come home and stay with us for a few days until you feel better?" With a breath, I replied, "If I don't go back to my home now, I will never leave your house."

Home, we came as a family with a new dynamic. Fear, tears, loneliness and uncertainty — it all kicked in when everyone left. I had no idea how I was going to cope, but I knew that there can be no defeat where you just stay focussed and make plans. It was not an easy run; I lost all my confidence and self-esteem. I was mentally and physically drained. It was around this time when I looked at building a vision board to help me move forward. I had heard of them, but I had never used them before. I also started to journal the thoughts in my head, filling in the white note pages in a day-to-day diary after each long day. This gave me a clear head to go to bed with and to write up my next-day family and business plan. I knew I was heading to court for a messy divorce with child access, so the notes helped me with dates, times, etc. I did not miss anything.

Eighteen months on, I was still juggling work, going to college at the same time to get my floristry qualification, nursery, and working all weekend on open markets. Mum, Dad and my sister Alison were helping with childcare so I could still work weekends. I was also still between lawyers and court about the boys' access to their father. It was mind blowing and I was just holding it all together but nothing more. My lawyer summed it up well. in a funny way, "Heather you're grieving for something you don't want but need, the support of your ex-husband." Little did I know then that I was about to experience another type of grief.

I woke up to a telephone call from my mum on Monday 29th April 2001 at 5.30am to tell me my brother Thomas had died of a heart attack. He was just 37 years old. Devastated not to say goodbye, I felt everyone was robbed of that precious moment. No one could answer why Thomas had been robbed of his life. He left behind two children, Chelsea and Jason, now without a father. It was so unfair. That telephone call changed my life and I have been telling everyone since. One telephone call can change your life. So, enjoy every moment you have.

My grief for Thomas taught me a serious lesson, a broken heart that can never be fixed but time may help the healing. However, the pain will always be there. I kept asking myself, "Why was I grieving so much for a broken marriage when I had choices?" I told myself to stop. I have choices. Sadly, I could not fix Thomas's heart, but I could fix my own. So, I realized that it was time to step up and get closure, get Nathan and Liam's custody sorted, and the divorce moving forward. This took 7 years, but it was part of the process as I moved forward with my life. I started to feel better one step at a time. I had a vision and a purpose and as I was the sole parent to Nathan and Liam. I took full responsibility for finance and parenting. I started working on self-doubt, I started laughing again, and I began going out with friends believing that there was a rainbow at the end of the tunnel. But just as life sometimes presents the unexpected, I was stricken by grief again.

My friend and neighbour, Tricia, died. Tricia and I had become good friends since Nathan and her daughter, Lucy, were born in the same hospital a day apart. We spent a lot of time together going to toddler groups, nursery, school runs, etc. Tricia was expecting her fourth child. She had 3 daughters and was so excited to be having a boy. She went to full term pregnancy, but a complication set in during delivery and although her boy survived, she did not. This really distressed me, and I was understandably angry. Why Thomas and now Tricia? I could not work out how two good, loving human beings were taken away so early, leaving young families behind. It was just not fair.

Of course, it was not just me struggling with grief at the time, others were struggling too. Thomas was my mum and dad's first born. His sudden death had taken its toll on both of my parents. The twinkle had left my mum's eyes, and with time she became unwell. They decided to go to Spain for a break but on their arrival sadly things got worse, and Mum needed to go to the doctor's. From there she was sent to hospital and within a short time my dad called to say an operation was needed. My two sisters, Fiona and Alison, and I flew out to Spain to discover that my mum had bowel cancer. It never crossed my mind that my mum could die, especially at such an early age. She was only 67 when she passed.

I always had a close relationship with my mum, so to be told cancer was destroying her body was just unimaginable. Watching a strong beautiful lady fighting the disease every day is heartbreaking for everyone involved. Not only had she lost her only son, but she also had another battle to fight. Mum held on to the end with dignity. Anyone dealing with cancer treatment is a "hero" in my eyes and my mum was certainly my hero to the very end.

My GP recommended that I go into counselling to help me deal with what felt like a whirlwind of emotion. She said I was compounding emotion and grief by trying to get on with things and having a, "What's next to get done?" approach to coping. I was keeping busy but burning out rapidly. I agreed to go for counselling, and we worked on my empty feelings and negative thoughts. It allowed me to become strong and when Mum passed, I could cope better. Mum played a huge part in Nathan and Liam's life. I knew I would have to be strong for them too. As part of my coping strategy. I decided to look for ways to help me focus my attention on something positive. I had run a few marathons in my younger days and always felt strong mentally and physically as a result, so I took action and signed up for the London Marathon.

I began training during the week and found a PT coach who in the past was running marathons in elite time. Unfortunately, I would never get to that standard, but I was just happy to finish the race and enjoy the atmosphere on the route. Well, it was bloody hard 26 weeks training! I trained 3 times a week with a coach in the gym and on the road, 2 days on my own running and I had 2 days a week rest. I prepared healthy food and drinks, did kit prep etc. It was like another job, but well worth the commitment. I challenge anyone to do a marathon!

Then I was given an opportunity to walk the Wall of China for the British Heart Foundation Charity. This positive step really helped me focus and step up. I felt I could now face any responsibilities I had or any difficulties that I may have to face. I had one main priority — to survive as a family. Although my method may have appeared outwardly selfish, it was not. I knew that I needed to sort my own shit out in my head to go forward. I knew that if I was strong, I could be strong for others too.

I have such a happy memory of sitting under the stars one night in China talking aloud to Thomas as if he was the brightest star in the sky. It really helped me let go of the grief and anger I had been carrying with me for so long. I had to learn to let go of "Why Thomas, not me?" and accept that he was gone. I had to allow myself to deal with the loss of my mum, my angel mum, that through all my shit, was at my side helping me with boys while I was at work. She never complained once. She was a strong, wise, wonderful woman. I wanted to set the same example for my children.

I had completed my floristry course while mum was ill and now, I was at a crossroads. I wanted to be a full-time mum and did not want to be working every weekend of my boys' lives. The market trader's life had changed. People had started buying flowers online. Although I thought working in a floristry shop sounded exciting, the long hours every day were not going to fit in with the nursery and the school runs. It was not going to be financially viable either. It was all so uncertain. Then I was given a copy of a book by Robert Kiyosaki and Sharon Lechter called, Rich Dad Poor Dad. It was a property book that opened my eyes to the possibility of creating a new stream of income other than selling flowers. If you have not read this book, I totally recommend you do. Wow, it simply blew me away. As a result of reading the book, I decided to undertake a 2-hour property seminar. This led me on to making a mega choice, to undertake a 3-day property seminar in Edinburgh, and I was not going to ask permission from anyone. I was going to do this for me and learn how I could create a solid financial future for my boys and myself.

That seminar led me into a world of motivation, empowerment, inspiration, focus, learning skills and meeting new people, people looking for the same things in life I was. I honestly did not know what I was looking for, but my gut told me to go along.

At the first seminar, there was a whole room of about 80 people. We listened to a speaker telling us how to purchase property in other ways, such as HMOs (home of multi-occupancy) B2L (buy to let), creative finance (how to raise funds), asset protection (how to safeguard your assets) and how to buy distressed property. I love education and learning so this was a no brainer for me. I went on to purchase a full program, the best funds I've ever spent. Paying for your education on whatever topic it may be and helping your self-development is money well invested in yourself.

I hired a mentor, Major John Dallas, a diamond of a man who shaped me into the businesswomen I am today. I knew it would not be easy but with the correct guidance, support, action and staying focussed to the end goal, I knew it would work. What's the saying? *Blood, sweat and tears but real determination*. I was buzzing for the first time in a long time. I had a focus! Finding a coach or mentor that you are happy to take direction from can really change things for you. Determination will get you to your end goal.

Over the next two years I worked from my kitchen table when the boys were at school. I learned everything about property. At the same time, I felt a bit trapped in the sense that property is a lonely business. Working from home is extremely lonely, not speaking to the outside world yet also being careful people don't take advantage by popping in and out when they know you're working from home. You also need to take yourself seriously enough that the business builds. I knew had to make changes to get a more structured life, so I opened my first letting agency in May 2008 on Baillieston Main Street. I went on to win the Landlord UK award 2010, 2011 and 2012. The location was perfect as Nathan, now 11-years old, and Liam, now 9-years old, were attending different schools. I wanted to be in a position where I could pick them up from school. One school was 10 minutes' walk from the office and the other was 10 minutes in the opposite direction. It was the balance we needed as I built the business.

Thankfully, I had huge support around me to help me do this. A dear friend of mine, Helen, who is also Nathan's godmother, and was my bridesmaid when I married in 2022, took on all the roles of babysitting and school runs initially, so I could travel for property education. I would then drop boys at school, open the office and leave at 3pm to pick the boys up to go to cadets, Tia Koi Do, football etc. Helen would close the office up. We had such a great supportive relationship, and she helped me build the letting agency. She is the most wonderful human being and has displayed such loyalty through all the ups and downs and to this day, both in my personal and business life. My boys adore her, and she is my number 1 side kick.

Another dear friend, June, my oldest friend from our first day together in primary school, also did her fair share of job-sharing, working on the market stall, and babysitting the boys. She started working with me the weekend after I lost my mum. She came to work in the office for a few days a week to do the rent collection. A true, loyal friend who I am so grateful for.

Elizabeth, my cousin, who is more like a sister, was also at my side from the early days of the market stall. She helped me out on Sundays and worked around her family commitments, which also meant I could leave early to collect the boys. Elizabeth even followed me into the office to become the office cleaner, and even came to my house on a Thursday to help me out. She made such a difference to everyone's life and is another true loyal wonderful human being.

Alison, my youngest sister, helped massively with childcare as did my amazing mother, my sister Fiona and my dad. They were all there every step of the way, with never-ending support to do anything and everything that needed to be done, no questions were asked. It was always "job done and what is next?" I could never have survived with all that love, care and support and I will be forever grateful for it. It allowed me to continue to work on my property education.

As part of the package from the Rich Day Poor Dad program I had paid for, I worked with another mentor called Debbie Rice. Debbie and I spent 3 amazing days in Glasgow going through my business and goals, a strategy, and what I wanted to achieve. I announced to Debbie on day 3 that I was going to become a mentor. So, the next level of my education was to become a mentor under the Rich Dad Poor Dad banner journey.

I had such a good relationship with Major John Dallas and later Chris Cormack, another great mentor from Edinburgh. We shared many an early flight to London from Edinburgh, always eager to help and support throughout my UK and international mentorships. At the time, the letting agency involved Helen working full time with Fiona, running the maintenance side and I simply took a consultancy fee. However, as the company grew, staff problems started. With people off sick, the company started to hemorrhage money. I was physically exhausted and on my way to burnout. I had a discussion with my coach and mentor and I made the decision that the letting agency was no longer for me. It had helped me through the period of grief in my life, but it was no longer my passion. I made the decision to sell, and I told everyone that the business was for sale.

One member of the staff wanted to buy me out but did not want to employ the maintenance team. I was resolute, it was a package deal or no deal. David, another letting manager, asked to come and work for me with the hope of buying me out 18 months down the line, which he did. With David in the picture, I could start working harder on property mentoring throughout the UK and internationally. I loved helping, motivating, and seeing property students moving forward on the correct path to financial freedom. It also gave me motivation to expand.

I started to build a sourcing company with John Dallas, and at the same time Rich Dad Poor Dad had opened the international side of their business. Chris Cormack asked if we would source property in Glasgow for international property students. John and I started travelling to London on Tuesday mornings, presenting deals to students from all over the world. I will never forget the 6am red-eye flight out of Edinburgh and then the 90-minute travel into Richmond London to present. We always just made the last flight home and then the drive from Edinburgh to Glasgow. We were so tired but so motivated and inspired, we never thought about it at the time. We had agents in Glasgow that brought deals to us. We sourced them on. We undertook their refurbishment and put them out for letting. That was how we built the business.

As the international market was growing, I was asked to attend events in Kuala Lumpur, Hong Kong, Austria, Paris, and Switzerland. I was speaking to hundreds of people, potential property students, educating them on being a sourcing agent and the benefits of building a property portfolio in Scotland. I simply loved the experience. I was asked if I would consider becoming an International Mentor within the group. The only stipulation was I had to "let go" of the sourcing and letting agency. Well, that was a no brainer! When it comes to choices, I am completely comfortable in my own skin. I decided to pursue the things we needed as a family, and for myself, without asking permission or worrying about being judged. I started a business that I am proud of, starting with nothing.

The letting agency is still operating today, with David and Kasia now the owners. Well done, Kasia and David!

I used my personal experience and channeled my insights into practical knowledge that I gained throughout my mentoring career, and now one of main goals is to bring to the attention of everyone that you can achieve your full potential with the right support of a coach and mentor at your side. You just have to be willing to make a decision and take ACTION! I try to recognize potential in all my students, regardless of their background, looks, financial status, position, or age. My youngest student, Liv, was only 15 when she and her mother Alison became my students, and both have gone on to do amazing things. Liv won her 1st award under me and is now a well-known figure under Liv Conlon Stager Boss. My oldest was an 82-year-old called Tracey, a lovely wee lady from Manchester who wanted to leave her wealth to her great grandkids by setting them up a property portfolio. This was all complete before Tracey gained her wings.

As a result of making the decision to survive no matter what, moving forward one decision at a time, I got my power back and I have since achieved so much that I am proud of, With decision and action I have completed 10 full marathons, completed the London Marathon 3 times and ran in numerous half marathons, I climbed Ben Nevis (the highest mountain in Scotland) 10 times, walked the Great Wall of China twice and climbed Kilimanjaro (the highest mountain in

118

Africa). I have also won numerous awards, such as the Letting Agents UK award (2010 - 2011 -2012), the Rich Dad Poor Dad Legacy Education award (2015). The Mentor of year award to the youngest student, Liv Conlon, the Business Women Connect Scotland award (2022), the best property coach (2022) and I was shortlisted as a finalist for the Make it Happen real estate category in 2023. I have also supported numerous charities, such as the British Heart Foundation and charities that help people with Cystic Fibrosis, Cancer, and Dementia.

Making a decision to survive and thrive is not always easy but take it from me, it is worth it! I have learned so much from my journey and I would like to share with you some of the things that have been instrumental to my success. If I was to sum it up as a recipe, this would be it:

Build a loyal power team around you. Write out who you need in your business and personal life and start vetting them.

Delegate. It's amazing what getting a cleaner or iron lady once a week in your house can do for your mental health.

TTP (Talk to People). Never be embarrassed to seek professional help. If you can't fix it yourself, don't waste time on being embarrassed and get the support you need. It is the quickest way to move forward in your journey.

Face that fear and do it anyway. I always ask myself what's the worst case that can happen, and if I can cope with that, great. JUST DO IT!

Ask yourself what is the best result that can happen. See your dreams becoming a reality.

Remember, with every cut and bruise, you will become one hundred times stronger. Like a kid that gets a cut or a bruise after a fall, they run to their mum until after a few bruises they get stronger and don't run back for a hug. We are no different in business and life; every time something goes wrong, we can get stronger by learning how to cope as we grow.

Every week or month take yourself to your safe quiet place. Make it so you have no distractions from anyone; put your phone on silent, breathe in fresh air and start on your journal and plan.

Write – Do – Review Make this a habit. Set clear objectives, put systems in place and allow for time management.

Be True to yourself: This is your life, do what makes you happy as you only get one chance.

Stay focussed on your WHY SUCCESS HABITS: Why do you get out of bed in the morning? Never forget YOUR WHY, it is the most important part of this journey.

Be Accountable. Set targets and hold accountable for them.

Affirm your Worth. Acknowledge your value and make the decision to be your best on a continual basis. Learn to say No when you need to. Avoid comparing yourself with others. You're unique! Build on your strengths and shift your focus from doubts to your vision.

Everything starts with a positive mindset and baby steps. Break done the bigger picture and be patient. You will achieve your goals!

Live Life Well. A Wise Man once said:
Hate has 4 letters but so does Love.
Enemies has 7 letters but so does Friends.
Lying has 5 letters but so does Truth.
Cry has 3 letters but so does Joy.
Negativity has 10 letters but so does Positivity.
Life has 2 sides, choose the better side of it.

It has been an absolute pleasure and honour working with Donna and all other co-authors. Thank you, Nathan and Liam, for turning out to be two handsome, independent young men. Thank you to my husband, Brian, for supporting me through challenges. My world, my family. WE SURVIVED!

Love and Smiles,

Heather x

CHAPTER 7

Victim to Victor

by Natalie Duffy

"If I didn't have bad luck, I'd have no luck". This was the way I used to think. Now, however, my mind frame is completely different. Now, I try to see the positive in every situation and if that's not possible I think, what is this tough time / lesson trying to teach me? If I could see me now in comparison to back then, I wouldn't recognize myself. Through self-development and investment, I worked relentlessly to change my attitude and outlook in life, although this was not an easy thing to do. I knew I wanted more from life, and I wanted to be "happy" so giving up wasn't an option. I learned to fall back in love with myself, take pride in myself and my appearance, work on my confidence and conduct myself in a manner I was proud of. Years on, I still continue to work on myself on a daily basis and know self-development is something I will continue to work on throughout my life. The first step is becoming aware of your mind frame and understanding the behaviours and coping mechanisms that you have learned and utilized throughout your life.

In my life, I was subjected to many situations that I had little to no control over, and over time my mind gradually surrendered to the trauma and chaotic reality. This chaotic whirlwind became normal for me, although deep down I knew it wasn't.

Personally, for me, my life began to spiral out of control at the age of 18. My son had passed away, my partner at the time was severely physically and emotionally abusive, I fell into chronic depression and addiction, and I felt I couldn't be honest or truthful with anyone in my life. To help myself manage and mask how I was really feeling, I self-medicated and allowed myself to get into a significant amount of debt, which further impacted my mental state as I was constantly under financial pressure and final demands.

I lived in a state of constant, all-consuming anxiety and fear, and I gradually became someone I didn't even recognize. I was 7 stone heavier than I am now, I was out of work and claiming benefits — I'd always worked since 13-years-old — I was in financial hardship and significant debt, and I was severely unhappy with my life; how I felt, how I looked, how I acted and how I behaved. I kept those I loved most at arm's length in fear that they would get to know "the real me", I had little to no self-care or self-confidence and never prioritized myself. My life consisted of getting by each day and never thinking of the bigger picture, just trying to get through each moment.

I was very angry inside. It was evident from the minute someone met me. I blamed the world for my problems, never reflecting on my own actions or responses. I was the victim of my own story and I felt I could justify it when I thought back to the situations I found myself in many, many times. I was angry in every area of my life, my physical health and appearance, my abusive relationship, my financial situation and my son's death.

I fell pregnant in my teenage years and was scared and nervous to become a teenage mum. Throughout my pregnancy everything was great, no concerns or issues were raised, and I believed I was carrying a very healthy little boy. I went into labour naturally at home, however when I arrived at the hospital, I was informed there were complications. This turned out to be a major blood clot that cost my son his life and severely impacted my physical health followed by organ failure. Following my son's death, I felt I couldn't see the wood from the trees, I tried to talk to professionals, however my mind frame didn't allow me to see it from a different side, look at it from a different perspective, or listen to anything that would allow me to heal. I couldn't fathom how I would ever be able to overcome my heartbreak, hurt and pain and lead a life of positivity, happiness or love. This was made particularly difficult by the fact that I was in an abusive relationship, and worst of all, I didn't see just how bad it was.

People close to you, in your circle or outsiders can point out the red flags that you don't see, but it's not always as clear cut as identifying the "bad" in a situation and then walking away. When you find

125

yourself in a bad situation, as human beings our heart tells us it can be changed, it can be worked on, or "they" will change. We listen to our heart in hope of a better future, a happier relationship, or a positive life.

Walking away from bad situations can be difficult and scary, especially when there is no certainty of a better life. You are walking away from something familiar and exciting in your comfort zone, which is daunting in itself. Family, friends and those in your life become aware of your current situation and it can be frightening to open up and talk about situations you may have hidden and buried deep down, believing you'd never discuss it with anyone. Staying in a bad situation can feel easier than letting go or walking away. You tell yourself it will eventually change, things will become better, and everything will be okay. Leaving a bad situation can leave you feeling lonely and vulnerable, and without a good support network or family this can be very difficult to deal with. I, myself, had an excellent, supportive family, however they were unaware of the challenges and hurt I was facing therefore it was very difficult to drop the barriers I had spent years building and allow them into my real reality. Even if it meant I would have support, it wasn't that easy, it took courage and strength to allow myself to be vulnerable in front of those I cared for most. I knew I wanted more in life, a better life, a life I looked forward to waking up to every day and living but when you feel like a victim it's easier to stay in what you know.

I then fell pregnant with my daughter, Emily, and I knew I didn't want to be the "fat" mum in the park and struggle to play with her. I had longed to be Emily's mum for so long, I wanted to enjoy every moment. I wanted to be a mum that my daughter would be proud of. I wanted to work and get back on my feet financially. I wanted to be a nicer person, treat people better, and not allow my anger and hurt to overtake my emotions and responses in difficult or confronting situations. I wanted to look and feel better. I craved to change, to be proud of myself, to get out of this lifestyle I had fallen into throughout my early adult life and create a life I was beyond happy and proud of, but I also knew that for anything to change, I would have to strip everything I was telling myself right back and look at it from a different perspective. Even regarding my weight, I blamed everything from contraceptives to physical health, never would I accept any responsibility or commitment to change.

Stripping everything back, accepting responsibility and facing the reality I was living and had created, either through choice or mindset, was the hardest pill to swallow. If it didn't scream victim, I didn't want to hear it, but in order for me to change I knew I had to stop telling myself lies and repeating my sad story in my head. I had to take a long hard look at myself, the areas in my life I wanted to change and be honest with myself about decisions I was making and what I was accepting, for if you're not changing something that makes you feel bad, you are accepting it. If you want to change you have to let go of a victim mentality.

127

There was no one better at playing their own "victim violin" than I was. I would replay my son's death, the severity of the abuse I had sustained at the hands of someone I once loved, what I saw in the mirror when I looked at myself, and my financial difficulties, over and over and over again until I was justifying everything. I was unhappy with my own life. I would begin to justify why I was so angry and how I acted and convince myself nothing was my fault. As my story went, I was always the victim, never the victor.

Mentally, I had to prepare myself for change, for a healthier lifestyle, to make time to invest in myself, to be honest about my life and relationship and accept the opinions of others, which was something that I struggled with, the thought of annoying or not being "liked" by this person or the next daunted me, so I'd have kept it to myself. The thought of people knowing my business and asking questions kept me awake at night. I knew I had to put myself first, put myself ahead of my fears and make some sort of change. I already felt I was living in Hell, so what was the point in stopping there?

I had restarted therapy for the 100th time, not very optimistic at all. During one of the sessions, I was asked to journal my feelings and behaviours and re-read them at a later time. I thought he was mad. I wasn't the kind of girl who sat down and wrote about how she was feeling and now I was being asked to do this daily. I gave it a go, for as I said, I was already in Hell, why stop now?!

To my surprise I loved it. I felt I got to write down everything I felt without having to feel vulnerable in front of someone else. I got to reflect back on situations and began to see how my trail of thought may not have always been correct. I got a better insight into why I was in financial difficulties, because my spending habits were atrocious and I prioritized my wants over everything else, because remember, in my reality, I was the victim.

Then I started a food journal, and it's safe to say it didn't take too long for me to see, in black and white, I was the problem, my eating habits, portion sizes and unhealthy snacks. Despite being massively overweight, it took for me to put it in writing to fully see where I was making bad choices and decisions. When it was in black and white in front of me. I was unable to deny it, whereas before I blamed everything for my weight gain other than my own diet and eating habits. It took for me to sit down and visually see what I was doing before it sank in. I realized when journaling and writing things down I was able to resonate with it, this quickly became my strategy for all areas of my life where I was unhappy. I started to tune into myself and my behavioural patterns and began to understand myself better. I now knew journaling and putting feelings, goals and plans into black and white worked well for me and I could utilize this to get me from where I currently was to where I wanted to be.

I began to write down my goals in life, break them down into individual steps and hold myself accountable. Sounds easy enough to follow right? Well, it wasn't that straightforward, I now had a strategy that worked well when helping me achieve my goals and get a better understanding of myself, however I still needed to change my way of thinking. I was still operating from a "glass half empty" perspective. Although I had found a successful strategy, my mindset was still not in alignment with my goals, and this had to change in order for me to operate at the frequency that would match the life I craved. As the saying goes, your frequency is what you frequently see, and I didn't like what I was seeing.

Accepting that my mindset was not right got me thinking, what else am I looking at wrong? What else am I only seeing from one side? Personally I had to look at how I acted when I found myself in difficult situations, how I managed my weight and made dietary choices, how I responded to abuse – react or respond, they are two very different things, my spending habits and how to get control over my life as I felt by this stage it had spiraled out of control and there was no salvaging it. It was easier to bury my head in the sand than to face the truth of my life and the choices I'd made.

It was a snowball effect for me. It started off as I would describe a square, and slowly but surely it got easier and easier to push until it was a rolling circle. I always thought I'd change it all in a day. Of course I will, I will just stop everything I'm doing and make different choices and all will be better, right? I couldn't have been more wrong. I had to work and work and work at it, many times giving up and again falling victim to my own story, my own reality!

I started taking one small step at a time consistently until I had it nailed down. Then the next small step would come. It was like learning to walk all over again, slowly put one foot in front of the other and watch your balance. Over time small steps turned into big changes. I had started to lose weight and keep it off. I wasn't going from 1-100 instantaneously in rage, I could see how I got myself into a financial hole and how to start getting out if it, I had the inner courage to no longer accept abuse of any form within a relationship and I was starting to enjoy the person who looked back at me in the mirror. I was now living by the motto of "become the source of what you seek".

Small steps make big changes when you are consistent, dedicated, and focused. These were 3 things that were big for me in changing my reality for I had never been any of them in the past:

- I had to be consistent in my daily decision making and show up regardless of how I was feeling that day.
- I had to remember why I wanted to change and be dedicated to achieving my goals.
- I had to remain focused of what my purpose was and throughout each day continuously ask myself, "Am I focused on my goals, is my attention where it should be?"

Numerous times I felt low, unhappy, full of self-doubt and negative self-talk, it wasn't just rainbows and sunshine once my reality began to change. It was paramount that I remembered how hard I had worked, and that Rome wasn't built in a day and that was okay.

I had an excellent support network around me, routing me on and I was very lucky, however the responsibility to stay focused and consistent was on me. Your circle of people is crucial to the kind of person you will be. I learned that you are the average of the five people you spend most time with, so it's vital the people around you are your people and want what's best for you. Albeit having a support network is important, the last thing you want is to develop a crutch and begin to depend on your supports in order to achieve your goals.

Stepping into the unknown is petrifying, it's uncomfortable, painful, and lonely, however in order to develop, grow and become successful it is of utmost importance that you exit your comfort zone. When outside your comfort zone, although it's scary, it will change you into who you want to be. You get the opportunity to meet new people, new skills, create multiple streams of income, participate in opportunities and build yourself up.

I was the girl who went from 1-1000 instantaneously, bad tempered some would say. At the beginning of changing who I was, I agreed

132

with myself, I would not react to a situation, problem or argument for two hours. After two hours, if I still felt how I felt initially, I could stand over my response, however if my response was initially to react angrily and I no longer felt that way, I had to reflect on my reaction and why I allowed this to trigger me. This was not easy to accomplish, I tried and failed many times before I was able to control my emotions. I continuously reminded myself of the bigger picture, what and who I was changing and striving for, and always reminding myself that I had a baby girl I was raising alone, and I was going to be her example of how to behave and what to accept from those around you. I never wanted my daughter to become the person I was, so as much as it was hard to accomplish, it was harder to live with the guilt of being so unhappy and her having to watch it. This helped correct my responses moving forward as I now had insight that my side or opinion wasn't always right. Who would have known!

After learning strategies, for example journaling my thoughts, feelings, setting goals and breaking them down into individual steps to accomplish them, I did this with all aspects of my life. I wrote down where I currently was, where I wanted to be and the steps I needed to take to get there, only this time I held myself fully accountable, focused, consistent and dedicated.

As I started to get my life on track, I learned to focus on the things I could control rather than what I couldn't control. Instead of worrying, I would remind myself to live in the now. I started going back to the gym and fell in love with it again. I loved how it made me feel and how I started to look. The gym kept me on track with my meals and helped me manage my eating of unhealthy snacks. I loved the social aspect of working out and the difference in my mind frame following a workout. I wanted to know if everyone knew what this feeling felt like, actually happy.

Since changing my mind frame from a glass half empty to a glass half full kinda girl, I am happy and content in my life and continue to work on all aspects daily. I do believe there is no such thing as "When I'm happy I will..." Happiness is a state of mind, and it is solely down to you as an individual to work on making you happy. It will always be a work-in-progress, once you're happy it's not a case of forever happiness. Consistency, dedication and focus will keep you consistently on your shit though and keep you working on your happiness! An extra motivation for me was I never forget who is watching...

CHAPTER 8

Fear to Freedom

by Tanya Cannon

How can you transform fear into freedom? There are so many ways big and small that I conquer fear every day. But there are just as many ways I strive to embrace freedom. It is a journey of transformation that began in my childhood, the place where my fears were born.

As a child I was always told to shut up, that I was never good enough, that I was stupid. I was an innocent little girl who learnt to make herself small to please everyone else and, most critically, to keep myself safe. As I grew up, I gradually began to notice that this was what was lacking the most in my life — safety. Lack of safety has led me to have, at times, crippling fear. The type of fear that seizes me and makes me paralyzed and emotionally numb. To compensate I learnt to be overly positive, or always joking and laughing, all in a bid to keep the peace no matter what situation I was in. This meant that my negative emotions such as fear, anger, sadness and worry were pushed aside, and I would disassociate to cope. I did not develop healthy coping skills, choosing often to make myself small instead of speaking up. I saw fear as my enemy.

The fear I felt was probably a combination of my own and other people's "stuff'". There was a lot of fear in the air so to speak, as there were issues with substance abuse in my family, and aggressive behaviour as a fallout from that. There was very little support to help me understand what was going on, so I sat in the confusion of it all. Instead of being helped to grow, I would get the blame for things that were beyond my control or understanding, and I would be punished. Expectations that I was never going to meet were placed on me each and every day, and often I was forced into situations that were harmful and damaging. I felt like I was the ball between the tennis rackets that were my parents, and I started to believe at some point during all of this that I was useless, no good, that I'd never go anywhere in life, and I was a nuisance. I had very little confidence. Sure, there was enough to fake it, with my overly positive attitude and my joking banter, but there was no self-esteem. I had no belief in myself, except when I made people laugh, so this is where I drew my validation from, and it shaped how I dealt with people for good and ill.

I believed I would never be enough, and I was pretty sure I would amount to nothing. So, I stuck to just making people laugh and feeling good, and I thought I felt good because of it. This sometimes led me into dangerous situations with people who hurt me, and situations that no one should ever have to experience and so my fears began to fill not just my home space but also the big wide world. All I wanted was peace. And I would try to get it by any means possible, even if it was at my own expense.

I taught myself to please everyone else, because by pleasing everyone else instead of me, I found I was able to keep a measure of peace. That peace was not there all the time mind, but there was enough to falsely drive me on to continuously forget about my own wants and needs. The fear that filled me was always there. I learnt that there were always terrible consequences whenever that peace did break. Not only as a vulnerable child but also as an adult. I still struggle with conflict, and I have to remind myself that I don't have to tip-toe around everyone.

I still remember myself and my siblings always walking on eggshells. I would always try to protect the younger siblings, to lift their spirits, care for them, and shield them from the harm I couldn't shield myself from. I have memories of hiding them under blankets so they would not have to see what was going on. In that role as protector, I never had to think of myself, so I didn't have to face the sadness within me. I shut down and blocked out a lot of what I was feeling so I could survive.

As I focused on managing my younger siblings' wellbeing, I didn't have to think of my own. Even though it was difficult and often heart-wrenching during this time when I was so young, it did give me a solid grounding to step into management and leadership roles as an adult. I had to learn early on how to step up, how to be accountable, even during times of fear. I learnt to be independent and draw on an inner strength.

As leaders, we have to think about the greater good, the bottom line, the well-being of others to have a successful business or to be the best we can be in a management position. I could say my childhood and all that it taught me has carried me into my adult life with great success, unfortunately it was at the cost of a little girl who never got to be, yet I really like the woman I have become, and I appreciate her for all she has been through. It has given me a great work ethic and that inner strength I developed through adversity and fear, has led me to my thriving business and life.

Work has always been a place of growth and transformation for me. Around 7 years old I began working in a local vegetable shop, owned by a family member, just so I could get out of the house. I was set to bagging fruit and vegetables. It felt good to be wanted and valued for something, so I really loved going to work. I didn't get paid, I was too young, but the treats and praise I got were all the pay I needed. It was here, in my little fruit and veg shop job, that I taught myself that maybe I did have value, I did have a purpose, and that not everything in the world was scary. I learnt here that I was likable, even loveable, so I always tried to be the most likable and most helpful version of myself even if I didn't feel it. This way I could make sure that I was always liked and loved.

The flip side of this, however, was that I would constantly crave positive affection. The places I received affection and positive responses only made me hungrier, starving even, for praise and love from the one place I was never going to get it — my father. This has been hard to acknowledge as an adult. I know that the need for praise and validation outside of myself came from wanting so badly for my father to notice me with kindness and love. Unfortunately, I was mostly only terrified or falsely hopeful. An awful combination of feelings that infected all of my relationships, whether I realized it or not. But it was all I knew and the fear of stepping beyond that held me back, even though I knew deep inside I had to do it.

There was so much going on as I grew up that was caught up in survival, I was never shown or encouraged to strive towards something better. Life was so in my face at home that all I could see was the terrible dysfunction that was hurting us all. While I was small, my dad was always drinking. He would often be away overseas with his job and when he was home, he would be out drinking all hours. When he finally returned, he would be shouting, roaring and vicious. My mother would get the blame for everything wrong in his life, everything wrong in the house, or with us kids. She would get the blame for just being alive.

As I got older, he started to include me in this blame game. I would constantly be told to shut my mouth and I was no good to anyone. This was difficult. I quickly learnt not to be excited when he was due home because you never knew what form he would arrive in. I was afraid of him, and I realized as I got older that I couldn't compete with his addiction or his anger. So, I decided to look outside of myself for direction, to sense what was going on so I could work out the best way to avoid negative situations, and more importantly see where I could find comfort and care. The comfort and care of others made me wonder why I didn't get it at home, and I thought there must be something wrong with me, so every time I found appreciation in other people, I felt a little less wrong and a little more loveable. I had very little fun as a child, unless I went to Dublin to visit my aunties there, my mother's family, who treasured us, and still do to this day. They gave me an understanding of family life, and real love and care. They gave me what I so badly craved — SAFETY.

We used to go to visit my mother's family every summer and it was always fun filled. We would do baking, treasure walks, and family meals, and I found a measure of real peace. My time there always gave me a regular routine that allowed me to feel safe, to sleep full nights and to experience love. The feeling of safety gave me the space to grow. Every time we went to Dublin and I had that treasured time, I would grow mentally, physically and emotionally. In the months we were there I saw a world that was not violent and loud. I saw a world that was full of love and joy, and I knew that this was what I wanted. That space would give me the strength to keep going year after year, and inspired me in the work I do today, running a successful company that is like a family, and is a safe space for its employees who I always try to support in all they do. Those summers of safety taught me that I had a deep resilience I could rely on and a deep desire to want to build something that was positive and fulfilling as I grew older. I learnt to value myself over those summers. It took a long time to truly understand that and believe in myself, but here I am today standing tall, knowing I am enough.

As I came to value myself with deep conviction, I realized I couldn't settle for playing small anymore. The turning point came with the loss of a baby. I was 4 months pregnant when I had a miscarriage from the stress and abuse from my father. It was 1991 and this was supposed to be a happy time as I was engaged to be married. Except my father disliked with extreme prejudice, my fiancé. I was terrified to tell him about the baby and the anxiety took its toll on my body and mind. I ended up in A & E and was admitted.

My father came to visit me in the hospital. Not out of concern. He was looking for any reason to go after my fiancé. He was violently rude to the hospital staff in a bid to gather any information he could use to fuel his rage and justify lashing out. I was heartbroken and embarrassed. Not long after that my fiancé and I parted company. I found out years later that my father had threatened him. It was such a sad and confusing time in my life, but the loss of the baby and my future husband because of my father, stirred to life an inner warrior woman who was not going to let anyone bring her down anymore.

In fact, I made a decision that I was going to show everyone just how amazing I could be.

In 1992 I went to work for a fantastic cleaning company in Galway, where I stayed for 15 years learning everything to do with the cleaning business. I also, because of great managers and training, learnt how to care for myself and vision goals and plans into reality. My time working for this company changed my life, my mindset and my belief in all I could achieve.

Until this time, I did not realize how intelligent, valuable, unique and capable I was. In 8 short months I went from being a supervisor to a manager of a team of twenty-eight staff who worked locations all over Ireland. I saw I had a great talent for interpersonal communication and for getting the job done over and above what was expected. I took initiatives to make sure all was running smoothly and that all of my staff were well cared for and, more importantly, advocated for. My time as a manager gave me skills to keep going onwards and upwards. I learnt incredible new words and ideas such as 'goals', 'vision', 'empowerment', 'leadership'. I developed a knowing that I can achieve anything I set out to do.

But then, I had a near fatal car accident in 2006. I was out for 16 weeks with a broken breastbone, and five broken ribs. During this time, I reflected on my home life and my work life, and I started to see a longing in me for something more. I acknowledged to myself that I no longer wanted to travel nationwide, I wanted to work here in my hometown of Athlone. It was a powerful time in my life that stillness and stopping. Even though it was forced on me by the accident, it inspired me to take the leap of faith in 2007 to start my own business. So, that year I gave myself a gift for my birthday, A1 Cleaning. Sixteen years later the company continues to grow and go from strength to strength as each goal I set, I achieve.

It was because I was not afraid to be still during my convalescence that I cultivated the space I needed to transform my life. That blessed beautiful space that I learnt to embrace as a child. The difference between then and now was that I could fully act on it and turn my world into one of joy, security and achievement. In setting up my business it gave me a deep sense of responsibility to myself, because it paid my wage, my mortgage and gave jobs to local people and put food on all our tables. I'm a girl of simple things and this was all the inspiration I needed to push forward and grow. Those things and feelings I craved as a child I was able to truly give to me, and it felt FANTASTIC.

I love to this day seeing my happy staff and happy clients, I loved doing my payroll (and still do) and paying wages each week knowing what went into earning them, knowing that my weekly goals were met. It gave me great confidence in myself and my ability to affect change in the world. I learnt how I could empower myself by making decisions and transforming my fear into something positive and from that creating freedom for me to be me, creating freedom financially and teaching me that I could speak and be my truth and still have peace.

I still have times that challenge me, that feel like I am being pulled back, and the old fears sometimes surface with these situations. How I respond to fear now is very different to the way it used to consume me and control me. Now, instead of letting it affect me to the point where I am afraid of the world and people and so forcing myself to be perfect all the time, I stand tall and don't let the victim take over. I have moved from victim to victor, and I keep reminding myself of that with positive affirmations, surrounding myself with like-minded people who support me and encourage me. People who can tell me if my choices might not be great but who still support and love me, and I know have my best interests at heart. With these people in my life, I have come to realize my glass is not half-full, its overflowing.

The truth and safety my network brings me has been important for healing my wounds. The transformation of my mindset has one 100% changed my life. I can now see positives in negatives and know that even difficult times don't last forever. I have learnt to speak up and speak out and to show others that it is safe to do the same, to be themselves, to communicate and grow. I have learnt also that my down time is really important, that being on my own in the safe, calm space of my home is vital to my wellbeing. It is in this space of stillness and quiet where I can light a candle and detach from anything that might have affected me throughout my day and also give gratitude for my life. It is in this space that I have learnt to mind and support myself.

Don't get me wrong, I don't have it all worked out every day, I often have Internal tug-of-wars that mostly focus on my own worth and lovability. I still have some beliefs that were forced on me as child that surface occasionally when I am triggered. They can affect me in big and small ways, leaving me anxious, or filled with a small niggle of doubt, or the old fears come flooding back and stop me in my tracks. I have wondered if I will ever be completely free of them, the difference now though, is that I don't worry about them as much. I see them and I acknowledge them, I ask advice, I seek comfort, advice or work with a therapist if I need it. Above all, I always work to transform what I see as negatives into positives. It has become a superpower of mine, that positivity. It is infectious, I can bring that positivity to any situation and turn a tangled weave of what can be seen as a disaster into something magic and beautiful. I have learnt that I can show up and BRING THE LIGHT!

It feels amazing and this is what I choose to put my focus into. I like the way it feels inside me when I do this and I like the way it lights up other people's worlds, through the community work I do, the way I have a ready smile and a laugh for everyone I meet, being ready to step up and help if its needed and creating networks of kindness around me. Those networks are my evidence in the world that I am doing good, that I am good. I am not the waste of space my father led me to believe, I am not less than, I am enough exactly as I am. My fears are now my gateway to freedom because I made a decision to stand tall and be proud of myself and what I am achieving and what I have overcome. I am joyful about the goals I have, and excited for the future because I KNOW I AM FREE.

CHAPTER 9

Adapting to Life as it Happens

by Ian Jackson

Growing up in the heart of the drumlins of County Down, Northern Ireland, our farm life began before the sun even thought about rising. Our way of life was hard work that started early in the morning no matter the weather and ran 365 days a year, no holidays or weekends off. I tended to the land and animals with my dad and even though it was laborious there was nowhere else I wanted to be spending my energy.

When I hit 16, it was decision time: school or work? For many, it's a tough call, weighing up whether to continue with education that may prepare them for their dream job or start earning right away. But for me? My mind was set on the farm, just like my dad and his before him. I was determined to work the land with my dad, the land that was in our blood. I can remember my last day of school like it was yesterday, the feeling of freedom and liberation from an institute that was no longer serving me and my goals. Walking out of those gates, I was ready to embrace the life I'd been dreaming of for so long. But then reality hit hard, as it often does, no matter what age you are! "You can't just work on the farm," my father said, his voice firm. "You either go back to school or find a job somewhere else. "My heart sank. My dreams, visions and goals just evaporated

147

into thin air in a matter of seconds. Reluctantly, I enrolled in a technical college, hoping to pick up a trade. One month was all I could manage. It just wasn't for me. Back to the drawing board, I guess.

I still remember the day I came home to find that my father had pulled some strings and landed me a job as a mechanic in an Austin Morris dealership in the heart of Belfast. "You've fixed enough around the farm, this should be a walk in the park," he said with a proud grin. And just like that, I became an apprentice mechanic, ready to take on whatever challenges the workshop threw my way.

Growing up on that farm, I was practically born with a wrench in my hand. Fixing machinery wasn't a hobby, it was a necessity for running a vibrant and active farm. If something broke, you couldn't afford to wait around for someone else to come and save the day. You rolled up your sleeves and got to work. But my foreknowledge of mechanicing didn't always sit well with the other apprentices. It seemed like they couldn't wait to see me make a mistake so that I could be taken down a notch or two.

Then, my luck changed when I landed my first real job. There was this one veteran mechanic, who let's say, was a bit of a maverick who took me under his wing. It was like a match made in heaven. He'd get the toughest jobs on the forecourt, and together, we'd tackle car issues that others wouldn't even touch. Those were the glory days, you know? But like all good things, it came to an end. My mechanic mentor had a falling out with the management and had to move on.

Suddenly, I was back to being the odd one out, the guy the other apprentices loved to see struggle. I had the mechanical skill set that didn't match my age and soon I would come to realise that this rubbed people up the wrong way. In every large garage there is a senior mechanic, who often is recognised and respected for their years of experience rather than their expertise. I had once again found myself in an environment that would not praise initiative and having the skills that most felt were beyond my young years. It didn't take long for a complaint to come in because I had once again raised my head above my station. Their solution was to move me across to a different foreman who made his apprentices do all the work then took all the praise for it. This is when I knew it was time for me to go. I couldn't take that toxic environment for long. I knew I had to find my way out and find a new place where I could really shine and prove my ability and value. Looking back, it was those rough times taught me more than any smooth ride ever could. They gave me the opportunity to stand up for myself and believe in my abilities. The negative environment is what motivated me to go after the next big thing, which wasn't mechanics. I felt ready to take on a new challenge.

I went on to apply for a job in commercial sales where I did what it took to make things work. I enjoyed meeting sales targets but wasn't 100 percent satisfied. Through the power of connections, I was introduced to a guy who was a similar age to me who had a radio wholesale business. It just so happened that I was with my mum visiting his mother and he popped into the front room to say hello. We got talking to each other and I learned that he had a radio wholesale business and offered to show me the warehouse. My eyes lit up when I walked into that warehouse, I could see my next challenge ahead of me. There and then I asked if I could buy stock and sell it. Deal done. I picked stock up twice a week and started off by selling to people I knew. The stock was stored in my car, and I showed some of my colleagues at the commercial sales site what I had to offer. I sold some products to them until I was stopped in my tracks one day by the sales director and asked to show what was in the boot of my car. The director was unimpressed by my side hustle and told me to stop selling while I was working on their site, or I would be fired. The problem was my car was my storage/warehouse.

A number of weeks later the radio business owner asked me if I could take a product with me for someone to pick up as they needed it quickly and it was a shorter journey for them to call and collect it from me in Belfast. Of course, this was the day that the director decided to do a follow up check on my boot. I quit before the manager could fire me. I had heard through the grapevine that I

150

could negotiate a full-time role as a radio sales rep, so I quit the commercial sales job on the spot to go and pursue that lead.

A week later, I had managed to squeeze the information out of my original radio business contact where the headquarters were based and chanced my arm popping in. By coincidence, I bumped into one of the directors and tried my best to talk him into giving me a job as a rep. A few days later he got back to me and offered me a job delivering orders and merchandising the stock onto allocated shelf space to a Cash and Carry group they had just secured this new client Holmes Cash and Carry, Northern Ireland based but 7 outlets in Scotland. I accepted on the agreement that I would be working towards a role as a sales rep. This was my dream job; I was everywhere in Northern Ireland, delivering merchandising shelves, getting to know the branch managers and in doing so was able to expand the range. But for me to able roam the countryside, in company vehicle time was my own, no one nagging me, this was the job I was made for. Over the next five years I shaped my own role in the company, setting up a completely new department allied with the motor trade and reaped the rewards of success.

They set targets; I busted them. They set higher targets; I busted them. It got to a stage where the company targets did not line up with enough reward and benefit for me. Once I hit this stage, I knew I had learnt enough and felt confident to move on and setup my own business. Looking back, it was a real pity more wisdom was not

151

applied from both sides. Twenty-five years later I wrote to the managing director of the business retired now of course and thanked him for teaching me the business without which I would never be where I am today. A few weeks later I got a very warm reply, I kept in touch with him and his wife until he died several years later.

My goal had always been to work for myself and setup my own business. Through my previous jobs I had proven that I knew how to do sales and I had a solid customer base that I could work with. One of my customers who owned several car accessory shops approached me to take over one of their failing branches as a business partner there would be a personal investment of significance required, they setup a Limited Company and bought the shares at the agreed percentage. This would be my first experience as a director/owner role. In the first year we took turnover from £60,000, to £134,000, the second year to £302,000 and third year to over half a million. After achieving this success, I came against the same old brick wall, earning too much. All the other branches were spouting that I must have been getting favour over them.

I decided it was time for me to officially go solo. I found that I could move quicker than others could catch up. I was more than ready to be my own master in my own business, however exiting a Limited company as a director is, it's not as simple as leaving your employment. I needed to get my investment back and resign. This did not go well, I ended up walking away with zero, I'd invested a large sum of money in this business, I'd increased turnover by 10 times, but they refused to buy me out. I was married at this stage with a mortgage and all the other challenges that go with making a new home. However, staying on would hold me back. In the years I was there I got to know the bank manager. I chatted to him about what I was thinking, and he offered to match 100% of whatever I put in with an overdraft. I tapped my dad for £8k and the bank put £8k overdraft to it, I was off.

I had the sales success and a customer base that I had kept warm, I just needed the product. Actually, I'd been working on that for about 3 months and already had a verbal agreement from two of the major suppliers they would supply me directly but on a cash with order basis. The next two years were busy, turnover year one was £240k, year two just over double. I was making very serious impact on my competitors, especially those buying from my same suppliers. That brick wall again! But this time it was different; I was the young guy in the way and the other competitors wanted my account closed. The company sent over a very well-dressed sales manager from the London office to terminate my account. Now at this stage I was buying over £500k a year from them, and they were going to close me down. This was a very sad day! It was a Friday, (why does trouble come on a Friday?), and it meant we had all weekend to worry about it.

Over the weekend I hatched a plan, there was a range of products this supper had that no one else in Northern Ireland bought, I'd quietly developed a massive market for them. So, I called the top man the one who sent the hang man over to me. The first few minutes were me blowing off a lot of steam, however, I'd make some good points and I sold myself and the benefits I could bring by getting this sector of products sold here in Northern Ireland (they were affecting sales of a new range in UK mainland). They were finding this range troublesome to sell in mainland, but they had order takers not salespeople. One hour later we were still talking, a good sign. I arranged to fly over and meet Geoff Clarke. We got on like a house on fire, did the deal and I was back in business.

I am delighted to add that Geoff and I still talk to each other even today. He is twenty plus years retired, and we laugh often about the hang man he sent over. Geoff has been a real mentor to me all those years, I'd even call him today when I get stuck. I have a name for the people I met on my journey, "People of Influence." "People of Influence" — there were many in my life and still even today.

A contact from Securicor that I'd known for years called me up one day and offered a car phone. At that time these were pricey (£2,000-£3,000 plus monthly line rental) my contact made me at a very attractive offer (£750). That car phone changed my sales business overnight. Installing that phone meant that I could achieve more sales within a day without being held up in the office. Without that phone I would've missed out on two significant orders in the first week worth thousands. I thought, if this works for me then it could work for other business owners just like me, I was calling with these people. This was the moment I had found my product, mobile phones.

Over the next few years, I spent my time building up my supply chain for my established customer base. I opened a warehouse with shop front in Lisburn as mobile phones became more accessible to small businesses and individuals. Of course, when you start to be successful you start to come up against (brick wall) competition. Despite that I became one of the top 5 suppliers of O2 in the UK. We had reached a thrilling high in the business and it was time to expand. In any business you must expand or die. Change with the market or leave it. I was spending a lot of time at exhibitions to find the right people to approach and to keep me ahead of the game. I went to Las Vegas every January for 21 years in a row and that was the vision. In the first 10 years of my mobile phone business, the UK was 5 or 6 years behind the technology in the USA. By going to the exhibitions in the USA I could see what my market was going to be in 5 years' time. I knew what was coming our way and I was the first one to have the products sourced to supply. The other gap in the market that I spotted through travelling to America was that UK phones wouldn't work once you landed in the States — remember this was 1990's. I made a contact in the States and bought phones out there and rented them to businesses in the UK to use while they were in America. I was the first one doing this and it was because of my eldest son figuring out the software logistics that we were successful in providing that product in the market.

The UK started to catch up more quickly with the USA's technology which meant we needed to adapt to the changing market again. The issue that now needed to be tackled was supply because the demand was there! This led me to approaching Nokia about a dealership, they were number one back then, as large as Apple is today. I was only a small fry. Motorola had already turned me down for an account, would I call them or not? I did of course, they could only say yes or no. I got chatting to the sales manager after a few days back and forward. He suggested I should come and see them at head office in Godmanchester, Cambridge, He added that we should leave it to next month. I wondered why but did not dare ask. The next month I went to see Chris, he was now the managing director of Nokia UK, wow! After a few hours of getting to know the range, we went out to launch and as we do over a meal the shutters are down and we get to know each other. It came to light that his wife is from Downpatrick, went to school there the same time my wife did and at the same school. He called Val, his wife, to ask if she remembered Gwen and she did. Well, that was the beginning of my business Dunmorris Ltd., being the sole distributor for Nokia mobile phones in Northern Ireland. This would lead to me being the envy of the mobile sector, that brick wall coming again? The sales of mobile phones were rocketing all over the UK. Through Nokia I had no supply issues and because I'd committed our business to promoting Nokia I was there number one client in UK, often stripping their stock of the shelves.

At this point in time Nokia was producing the smallest sized mobile handheld called the "Cityman" and their supply was reliable. As I'm sure you've experienced though – technology is not indestructible and the next hurdle that provided me with business growth opportunity was mobile phone repairs. As mobile phones were starting to be more widely used this meant devices needed repaired. At the early stages the only repair centre was in mainland UK which meant there was a long wait to receive repaired devices. I contacted Chris again, the Managing Director of Nokia, and asked if they would consider setting up a repair centre in Ireland. He brought it to the board in Finland for approval and I was given the go ahead. I asked the key question "what is it going to cost me?" and he said "£100,000 for the equipment, then you need to find the people and get them trained." This side of the business paid for itself fairly quickly and it set us apart and excelled our reputation.

My mobile phone business was well established and successful, I had the foresight to see how the market would change and had the repair centre setup via Nokia. Remember what I said earlier though? When you're on the road to success that's when the competition can come after you. Unfortunately, I could not predict that my competitors would come from within my own business. Around 15 years into the business I had set off on my summer holidays to Canada with my family and on the first day I got a call from Number 2 in charge at O2. He said "Ian, I'm sorry to call you on your holidays. You're not going to like this call, but you need to know. Two of your managers have contacted us this morning for a direct account to supply them because they are opening a new shop, and we think they're going to be opening it in your old premises." I replied, "Thank you very much for the call, I appreciate you letting me know." He continued to say "From our side, it's not going to happen, we are not going to give them an account. Just thought you'd like to know that."

My next call was to my travel agent, and I got a flight out of Canada that night. As I set off to head back, I contacted my trusted business mentor (who I still work with to this day) to ask him to pick me up from the airport. We went straight to my shop (my name was still on the lease), and we caught them in the act of setting up their business in my shop, also they were downloading my customer base from our mainframe – stealing company assets. We collected the keys to their business cars, asked them to leave the shop and had them up in court within a week. I was so fortunate to have the strong business relationship with O2 to have been tipped off about what was happening and catching the boys in the act. As soon as I received that phone call from O2 there was no question in my mind, I had to go back right away, or I would have missed my opportunity to confront them.

The billing companies like we know today such as EE, Three, O2, and Vodafone, were really network builders in these days and not all were billing calls to the customer, they would find third parties to carry out this facility. It was very completive and one of the new players in town back then was RSL Com. Robert S Lauder the son of Estee Lauder the perfume manufacturer. They approached us with a deal to take business away from Motorola, the deal was very rich indeed, so rich it could be too good to be true. Due to the pedigree of the owners, I went ahead. It accelerated the business to a new level in numbers we could now match larger competitors and often beat them.

Even after three years dealing with RSL Com I was unsure that the big pay day would come, and it did not. I got a very official letter from them that there were going to be changes in the business, two days later a letter from the receivers. I had built up cash bonuses just under £250k and it was gone, a much more immediate issue was we were not able to connect phones, and the two thousand plus we had running on the RSL Com network were not working. Nightmare or what!!!! How do we fix this????

I had built great relations with fellow dealers throughout the UK, there was only me in Northern Ireland. One top player in Shropshire that I knew very well called me, the next morning. He had been able to get a spreadsheet unofficially of all the dealers and how we were performing. There were five big players and to my surprise he said you are number 3 on this list. He went on to explain he knew the top person at O2 in the network side, I plan to call him he will already know RSL Com are down and share our numbers and see if he can help. I had a call booked in an hour; I said go for it. Late in the day, 8pm, O2 had agreed to take us five dealers on directly that was not done back then O2, only supplier brokers not dealers. They would honour the deal we were getting with RSL Com but not the big bonuses. We had every one of the two thousand plus people connected in three days and we were able to connect new sales as well.

The experience with the two employees going behind my back and trying to setup their own business was incredibly stressful, and on top the failure of RSL Com would take its toll. Three months after, it was at this point that the stress became overwhelming, and I was in a bad place. A trusted friend called into my office not long after this and told me I needed to go see a doctor. He setup an appointment with his private GP that afternoon and I was signed off with stress for 6 months.

We had an excellent acting managing director, Paula, come in to steer the ship whilst I recuperated. She found and employed a quality general manager that meant there was a layer of management between me and my staff which took a lot of pressure off me. I did a phased return to the mobile phone business and a few years after that BT Plc (British Telecom) made me an offer on the business that I couldn't refuse, and I sold it to them, all 42 staff and 7 outlets in one afternoon.

Throughout my career I had been buying a property a year since 1974 but I knew that I didn't know enough to step out and do this full time. During the 6 months that I stepped away from the mobile phone business I researched the best mentors and training programmes for property investment and that lead me back to the USA. I spent a year with Dolf DeRoos, a property investment expert in Arizona which was around a £20,000 investment. I had just sold the mobile phone business to BT, and I believed this was an investment worth making, I have never once regretted this investment in myself. This programme taught me that I need to find homeowners who needed to sell their properties quickly so that I could make an offer below market price. Within 18 months I had bought over 350 properties. The only reason this was successful was because I sought out the most successful people in the field who had proven success in the field and learnt from them. Taking the risk to invest in the learning and training has been the key to my success in the property investment game.

In my vast business experience, I have learnt that you need to find trusted experts in your field and learn from them, this is how I have been able to adapt to life as it happens. Even during the most difficult days I have fought to keep going and have built a team of people around me that I can trust to give me advice that will help me succeed. I've been through the worst days of business and the best days of business and those are the ones that see you through to the other side.

There is always a price to pay for success, even Richard Branson paid a massive price to overcome British Airways in their mission to expel his competition. No one ever won a gold medal without fighting through the pain. The key is to look for wisdom and grace and respond graciously.

In my walk in business, I've relied on people of influence for help, they often had more wisdom and delivered difficult teaching with grace. They are priceless, be sure you hold onto them. I do.

CHAPTER 10

Embracing a New Reality

by Charles Eder

"Without change, something sleeps inside us, and seldom awakens. The sleeper must awaken."
— Frank Herbert

At the end of the school year, in 3rd grade, my parents, both international civil servants, prepared to send me to Germany to visit my grandparents. This had now become a habit, and my younger sister and I had no qualms about flying alone from New York City to Nuremberg via Frankfurt, every summer. After all, this was the third country I had moved to by age 5. For the first time, however, things were to change, radically. As the summer vacation drew to a close, we were told we wouldn't return to the USA. We were going to Africa.

On the one hand, this was exciting, and I was looking forward to untried foods, a new playroom, and even wiser teachers. On the other hand, I hadn't been given the possibility to say goodbye to my friends in New York. This turned out to be emotionally devasting as I had formed very close ties with many in my class. (Many years later, Facebook gave me the possibility to heal that wound as I reconnected with almost everyone from those times.) In terms of growth, this change was mind-blowing, as I had to accept many new realities that transformed the way I related to others, myself, and even with a higher spirit.

Only two years later, we undertook another soul-bending trip, this time from Dakar to Addis Ababa. Ethiopia had just undergone a Marxist Revolution and received massive aid from the Soviet Union and its allies. The emperor was deposed, imprisoned, and killed, two years before my arrival. The country was violently united under a new ruler and was in a constant state of security alerts, with roadblocks, large posters of Karl Marx, Lenin, and Friedrich Engels, defiantly facing the city's main square, and 10,000 Cuban troops camped outside my school. As part of the government's terror campaign, strict curfews between midnight (at times 10 pm) and 6 am (later 5 am) as well as armed fights in the city, leaving dead bodies in the street, were constant realities. One could wonder why anyone would have their children play and grow up in that environment by choice. Like so often, however, this context led to more self-reliance, maturity, and tolerance than a less adverse and more controlled surrounding usually promotes. Shared awareness by my school friends, family acquaintances, and local Ethiopian contacts, enlightened me about geo-political forces that engulfed newsreels and large parts of the world, as well as filling me with unease and developing a sense of courage necessary to stay safe. Nature also had a go at me, as I developed a great joy for spicy foods, curiosity about large aggressive ants, spiders, and a multitude of other, not always friendly, creatures, as well as mental strength with an active outdoor life in sun-drenched climes. Driving past dead bodies and learning about others' difficulties, with no end in sight, made me realise that what we often see on TV was my reality. Very quickly, too, I was confronted with teenage truths and new opportunities that come at that age.

I was both a sensitive and a very curious child. In adulthood, this often made me aware of my surroundings intuitively but didn't always lead to easy communication with others. However, awareness didn't always equate with acceptance. When I listened to friends and family describe an incident, such as a killing, or other reality in the news that I had also lived through, I became aware that not everyone will understand your realities, and sometimes not even their own, as these are impacted by a greater momentum, outside of ourselves. Commonly, I accepted that people's actions, especially those of younger ones, were driven by traditions, holding status, and role models. I was intrigued by the more rebellious friends, aware that reality wasn't of their dreams. I was aware how dressing, acting, and speaking differently was the rebel's way to search for acceptance while they didn't accept what reality offered. Some form of rebellion also impacted how those around me made decisions and recognised opportunities. As I was often the youngest in my class, I now felt I was catching up to be aware of what I, and older friends, accepted.

I observed that finding what to admire about others made me aware of more opportunities and brought a better understanding of differences. Quite early, I listened to fortune tellers (not always of the card or astrology reading type) as a kind that gave us better systems to follow than scientists or politicians, both rewarded by society for dealing with the unknowns. I'm not referring to acceptance of some mystical sayings and foreboding; I was interested in people like Alvin Toffler and those focussed on deciphering what is, what was, and what will be. It, no doubt, gave me comfort to know that even in turbulent times, with many hard-hitting, uncontrollable events, we could distinguish patterns and open the debate to new, better, and freshly welcomed paths. Today, the practice of futurists is everywhere but as I grew up many were still sceptical about this activity, and it was new.

Therefore, accepting that things will always be different (some say they'll change), is an easy way to become aware of changes. For many, this isn't comfortable or natural. I remember babysitting as a teenager on December 31st. I was so excited about the start of a new year that I once woke up a young child to enjoy the fireworks outside. The child just wanted to sleep. What is exciting and different for one, isn't natural and accepted by another. At another New Year eve's event, I was with numerous teenagers at a very nice home in Italy. Alcohol was everywhere, and adults were away, but not one person was drunk. How different from other teenage events where so much time was spent getting alcohol, only to get drunk.

Another time, I was working in Rwanda and a colleague was stopped, beaten up, and jailed for not immediately halting while the President's motorcade drove by. I knew this colleague well; we shared a house. I just couldn't imagine her being a threat to a fly, even less for the President of Rwanda.

Sharing these examples, I'm looking to point out that anything you or I consider as good, successful, or even healthy, can be 'switched'. We follow this 'switching' (awareness and acceptance) as we go from one side to the other numerous times in our lives. It could be construed as paradoxical when we accept something as bad is now considered good, and then switch again to accepting it as bad. This switching is another example of accepting a new reality; the awareness and acceptance cycle happening again and again in so many tiny areas of our lives.

When you're aware that something will change (or is changing), is that the beginning of your journey of acceptance? It rarely is. More often than not, we seem to accept the multitude of tiny, almost daily, changes, become aware of them, now start accepting all the discomfort and new dangers, become aware of these, and then either let go of any resistance to the change, flee the change, or we try to change the change (not always realising the irony in that act). Some games force our hand to accept change with the roll of a dice, ownership of a card, or the move of a pawn.

Being an avid chess player since a young age, and school chess champion at age 12 (my opponent was 18), I saw how a little move or missed move could have large consequences later. It was also clear to me that many small steps could lead farther than a few large leaps.

When my family moved from the USA to Senegal, a predominantly French-speaking country at the time, my father asked me, and my younger sister, whether we preferred continuing in an English-speaking school or not. My sister expressed no preference and my father, as if to complete an initial social experiment, registered her for the best-known primary French-speaking school. I was adamant about continuing with Americans and was placed in a missionary school much farther away from home. It wasn't clear to me immediately; how different my sister's and my schooling would be and what this separation could mean. At the time, I thought mathematics, history, and other subjects were mainly the same, only the language they were taught in was different. I was so wrong.

Though I was confident that my sister and I had similar potential, she turned out to be far better manoeuvring the corporate ladder and I was much more entrepreneurial, to point out only one of many differences today. What was clear to me, was that my school was much smaller and my initial class, 4th grade, had the same teacher as the 3rd grade. When I moved to 5th grade, we shared the same classroom and teacher as the 6th graders. There were 4 in my 5th grade class and our schooling was based more on our abilities and interests than our age or grade. Being good in mathematics, meant I was following the 6th grade course and homework. School was no longer about grades and rank but about presence and engagement. This new mindset would follow me for the rest of my life. Ever since I have been much more involved in extra-curricular activities than most of my fellow schoolmates and sister. Noticing more and more little separations between my sister's choices and mine, wasn't interesting at first, but only after the 'first-time' effect disappeared.

We're all prepared for the first time and yet the way we're prepared can be through fear or excitement. There's a way I've always enjoyed travelling and that has been to read as much as possible about my destination and then throw it all in the bin and tour my destination wherever it took me, with no regard to a list of to-dos. After all, I could be doing exactly the same as what the book, audio, or documentary guide said, but my physical and emotional reactions would be very different from the travel writer. However, though the travel guide is never what we experience when on the road ourselves, trying to replicate the very feelings expressed by the guide can be one of the joys of the tour. For example, if reading about the history of a place, travelling like a 14th-century monk, or a 16th-century explorer could be more interesting than seeing the city or country as it is today. Why should the past and its known ways not bring similar joys to those described in the latest travel guide? What would you do if you had to explore a place like an 18th-century cook, instead of a hungry modern man and woman? Or think of budding painters learning their trade by going to the Louvres and copying a masterpiece. Our understanding of the past is our door to our 'first times'.

I've sometimes found more joy in telling someone that I felt the same they did than in making a point that my experience was so different. Just like the water that flows under the bridge is never the same, so, every time I express my experience, I add to it or can even change it.

One of my most difficult experiences was to 'become' French. Although I was, officially, French, I didn't realise the impact of culture until I 'lived' through it. At 17, I was more likely to succeed as a student in the USA, the UK, or Germany. Yet again my father asked me where I'd like to study and this time, I said France. This is another crossroads for life direction. This may have simply been curiosity, but I felt that education didn't simply come from universities; it especially came from the total immersion in the unknown. Again, I didn't realise

how distant growing up American or British can be from growing up French (and the other way around). This wasn't another ERASMUS programme. Although my friends and teachers in high school were from all parts of the world, and we all figured out that with our outlook and willingness to put effort into all we did, we'd eventually succeed anywhere, this isn't how it works.

A huge amount of humility and introspection is required before one finally morphs into a more beautiful being, happy and fulfilled in another situation or culture. That, for me, is the real 'first time'. The first time to kiss, eat bats, swim, or rock climb, is infinitely smaller in dimension than a full immersion in another culture or understanding. Every notion of accepted knowledge, values, effort, success, and even beauty, are questioned and can be turned on their heads when fully moving from one culture to another. It may even be more challenging to move from one similar culture to another, than from diametrically opposite cultures, far removed in space. As an example, learning Chinese as an English speaker may be, after the initial hardship, easier than learning Spanish as an Italian, with the added inconvenience of never being able to clearly separate the two cultures as they have so much in common, and always risking some slight confusion.

When dealing with the reality of the first time, lest we forget, more often than not, we have to jump into a pool and then learn to swim. The 'first' isn't swimming but jumping into a pool. Swimming then follows. When making life-changing decisions, think about what the true 'first' is. In the next example, my true first isn't investing, but spending money. Some know how to earn, some know how to spend, and a few can combine both well.

One of the most frightful "first" decisions I made was when I realised that I was extremely spendthrift until very late into my twenties and I wanted to change this when living in Senegal. I hardly spent anything, and people would constantly come to borrow money from me, even the CFO/Payroll manager of an organisation I worked for did so. She told me about employees wanting an advance on their salaries and whether I wished to help as every month the organisation was keeping my saved-up money. (I hadn't opened a bank account in the country yet, not knowing if I would stay for long.) I had no issues with my money being used to help my co-workers. Senegalese colleagues were paying for weddings, funerals, health bills, education, and much more, with the money I saved up. Every month the CFO would deduct money from the employee that had 'borrowed' from me and I would get paid back as she deducted some pay from the borrower. (The borrower needed not to know the money was coming from me so as not to be faced with colleagues asking me directly.) Inadvertently, knowing that by saving up money I was making a difference, probably led me to save up even more. Of course, this kind of trust and informality is gone from most other places in the world, certainly from Europe or North America. You would need everyone to sign agreements and have other measures to ensure the workings of such a system. But my learning and fate came later, as I wanted to understand what it meant to spend money. I was going to accept that not all my money decisions were good and that I would be able to live with losses. This attitude, of course, has devastating consequences almost anywhere. I was not immune from these. As I started to learn how

172

to spend and invest, I made poor decisions several times. My first time changing my money habits had great consequences.

There are many firsts in life. What can be powerful is realising that 'seconds' (not as a unit of time) are a consequence of firsts and should be even less underestimated. Ask yourself, "Have I done this before?" What happened? Most poor decisions I've had to accept were when I wasn't dealing with an initial poor decision that I repeated again and again. A poor decision once is rarely cause for much upset. It usually enriches life as our understanding of reality grows.

The aim is therefore to know how to stop a poor decision immediately and how to repeat a good decision continuously.

Too often, we believe that our reality and our understanding (Weltanschauung) are forged by truth. If we see something, smell something, or hear something, then our senses are immutable. If our senses are wrong, it's because we've been tricked, manipulated, or have no experience, so we believe. As a result, we can make poor decisions. Fine-tuning our senses and awareness puts us in a more powerful position.

As a young student, I lived in a small building with two studios per floor. I was on the third floor, and, at one point, I was asked if I wanted to be the contact person for the management company when dealing with our building. This gave me the possibility to get to know all my neighbours, including a late middle-aged woman living just above me. One day, I received a loud knock on my door shortly after 6 am. A stranger told me the building was on fire, fire services had been called, and I should leave the building immediately. My first instinct wasn't to leave but to understand where the fire was. I was told it came from the studio above me. I quickly ran upstairs, still half dressed, and went into the studio. I knew the lady upstairs and was concerned that she may have inhaled smoke and was unconscious. The smoke was so intense that I couldn't make more than one or two steps into the studio. I ran back to my place and found a towel. I was hoping a wet towel would cover my face enough for me to go to the lady's bed and wake her up. I knew her place and knew the overall set-up well. I was still not able to make more than a few steps into the studio. By that time the fire services, followed by the police, were on-site. My worst fears were met when I was told that the lady was in the studio. What came next, however, upset my belief in my senses. The police asked us to wait around (there was only one other person that had stayed overnight in the building) and we were asked to come to the police station. The upstairs lady had had her throat slit and the fire was a cover-up of the crime scene. Being inexperienced with this, I could only think that the visit to the police station was for our safety and to get any witness report.

While waiting to be interviewed, my neighbour and I discussed if we had noticed anything. Suddenly, it dawned upon us that we both heard someone scream 'help' three times and then dead silence. I had looked out of the window when I heard the screams but hadn't seen anyone. I went back to bed thinking it may have been a playful scream, as I was in a very busy street with nightclubs and restaurants.

My neighbour and I also realized that the murderer had waited in the building for over 6 hours before setting the studio on fire. Since then, my senses and acceptance of truth, have made me aware very differently. I have been the first to report an emergency incident 5 times, including a death, two major fires, and a serious car accident, although many other passers-by witnessed the same. My senses and my reality changed, and I may no longer be able to go back to the previous state.

No matter what your preferences are, in terms of how you'd like to live, being open to the unexpected is the best way to live on your terms. Learning to come to terms with it can bring a sense of calm.

Our forefathers have passed on unsolved complexities of life to us. Often, they've also shared coping mechanisms to deal with these. When our forefathers were able to solve a complex phenomenon, it was passed on as 'reasoned', understood, and fixed. As if a calm-inducing gene had been passed down, our senses picked up new vibrations. For instance, we saw the sun move in the sky every day and stars shine in different parts of the night sky, and this led to unsolved complexities being passed on from one generation to the

175

next. Only when we 'understood' certain workings of the universe did we inherit a calmness about happenings out there that our forefathers didn't have. Other things remain unsolved and direct our fears and expectations today.

I remember the many anxiety-forming stories that filled papers and news reports about emergency and utility services breaking down as we reached January 1st, 2000. To show how unprepared the IT-dependent world was for a millennium date change, one report mentioned a Swiss man receiving a letter that he hadn't gone to school after his 6th birthday. In fact, he had just celebrated his 106th birthday but the ever-present and hard-working Swiss administration still had computer programmes with personal files allowing for two-digit ages (max. 99 years old). Embracing change seemed to be at another level when it involved large administrations.

At the time, I had already worked for large administrations, including the UN, and was beginning to understand how, if quickly repeated, a mistake was rewarded more than the questioning of a process that had top executive approval. If large organisations are piloted by top executive decisions, what is meant to correct these? Up till now, it seemed to be mainly political forces, the justice system, and fashion. To keep their positions, top executives would swim with political forces, shield themselves from justice, and seek to predict or shape fashion. Their longevity, and that of the institutions they led, which successfully moulded the millions they were to serve, could impact our need to accept change. As we, those moulded, avoided swimming against strong currents, we found more time to while away in pleasant pools that formed along the way.

Every time top executive decisions are kicked in another direction, this can lead to regular instances of lost control for millions and the need to question what we value (e.g. global financial crisis, COVID-19). One of my first jobs came from an MBA report for a small UK technology company on the rise. My international skills were used to find new markets for the products the company made. Although it took a long time to get new contracts, I was very active all over Europe and was very visible in exhibitions and other events. Our competition saw me present again and again. What I didn't realise is that we had caught up and overtaken our main UK competitor in the British market and my presence signalled that we were ready to overtake them internationally. Within six months, our UK competitor, the market leader for nearly 20 years, came with a takeover offer that was accepted by my company's Board. Presence was the lever that made a powerful market player seek familiarity with a takeover offer.

As I was growing up, my father enjoyed showing me the latest gadgets and tried to get me familiarised with them. It was a fun time and I'd delve into electronics, new tools, and new ways to solve something, all the time. As such, we were both on the lookout for what was new. This has helped me often in life as I changed countries, jobs, and social environments. I would often notice something new before others. While I wasn't in an environment for as long as some others, I detected trends or habits that prevented adapting to newer or better ways of doing things. If you can feel comfortable and "familiar" with what is odd or different, in an exciting new way in your environment and life, you'll enjoy embracing new realities much more as you travel with time. When you recognise the new and unexpected as inevitable, adapting is easier. Not only that, but opportunity also becomes apparent.

There's a sign that was present in France at almost every dual railway crossing: one train can hide another. (If you see a train coming from the left, another train may be coming from the right very shortly after. Don't speed across the rails after the first train has rushed by.) Opportunities are often the same. Missing an opportunity can mean missing a second, third and more opportunity.

Like a Russian doll or an onion, you won't see what the linked/dependent opportunity is until you seize the first one. In the past, people who knew me well commented on my sense of speed. Why was speed important? We get lifted by the most promising opportunities in a very short space of time but piled down with less interesting opportunities that always seem to move slowly.

I've missed many outstanding opportunities, such as doing a fully funded PhD in a world-class university, landing a very rewarding career with the next CEO of a large company, or enjoying the beginning of a political career with excellent mentors. At the end of the day, these opportunities reflect on where I was at a certain time in my life and who surrounded me. But they never defined me. Whether I successfully seized these opportunities or didn't, I had reached that level where it was possible. As you progress in your lives and focus on more and more understanding and better, more mutually rewarding relationships, you'll reach levels that open opportunities for you. Keep at it and be yourself. Two of the most powerful sayings, that have kept me going when reality was tough, are:

- Always do the small things in life like the big ones, so that, if God wills, you can do the big ones like the small ones
- Life isn't about going from success to success but enjoying the times between one fall and the next (It's the principle of learning how to ride a bike)

We are more plant than animal in our growth. Animals must act as predators or prey. Plants don't usually devour each other. They grow stronger as they attract more nutrients, find sunshine, and collect water. We shouldn't see our lives as victims to predators or as being predators ourselves. In the plant analogy, find the sunshine, open up to more nutrients, and protect yourself from situations that can dry you up.

179

"Yesterday I was clever, so I wanted to change the world. Today I am wise, so I am changing myself"
— Jalaluddin Mevlana Rumi

CHAPTER 11

A Life That Makes Your Heart Sing

by Ashleigh Tobin

Has it ever happened to you? You're rushing around like a headless chicken, but you never actually "get-on-top-of" things. Maybe you've been going full throttle for a long time now and your body feels like your reserves are running low. You wake up feeling like you've been run over by a bus most mornings and coffee, sugar, or a combination of both, is what gets you through the day. As a result, you have brain fog - you're forgetful and distracted and find it hard to focus, especially at work. And some days, especially in the afternoons, it's as though someone has pulled the plug – you feel drained and exhausted, and it can come out of the blue. Then, the irritability kicks in and you hear yourself get tetchy with a work colleague or you're irritable with a family member and then you feel guilty or bad inside. The reality is there's probably not much 'wrong' in the bigger picture of your life. Sure, you're busy, but life is good, and you know that others have it so much worse than you. Yet, you find yourself wondering what the hell happened to the person you once were and if you'll ever feel like yourself again.

This was exactly how I felt many years ago and I wasn't sure why... on the outside, I had it made. I was in a senior leadership role in the pharmaceutical industry, and I was good at my job. I was happily married, had a lovely home, and a young daughter with hopes for more children to come soon. I was earning a great salary that allowed bills to be paid, plus holidays and savings, so our future looked bright. But on the inside, I was exhausted, regularly close to overwhelm and running on empty. It seemed that no matter how fast I tried to "catch up", there was always more to do. And my mean internal critic told me I shouldn't complain because my life wasn't that bad compared to some. But it felt pretty bad to me. My long working hours meant I had very little time to spare - I could stay on top of work and of my connection with my daughter but there wasn't a week that went by that I didn't hear myself say:

"I'll do that later…"

"Maybe someday…"

"When I have more time…"

"After this project is finished…"

"When things settle down…"

"Once I get on top of things…"

Someone else's urgent.

Have you ever heard yourself say these things? I wondered if it was only me who felt this inner discontent. Was this how life was meant to be? Was I the only one struggling to keep up? Everyone else looked like they were on top of things. What was wrong with me? It felt as though somehow life was passing me by. Surely, it couldn't be "normal" or "okay" that the only way to stay "on top of things" was to constantly go at full speed? I heard this unrelenting whisper that 'there must be something more,' which left me questioning my values and the people and tasks that were getting most of my time. No matter how hard I tried, I could never keep up with the standards I had for myself or the ever increasing To Do list I thought would help me achieve more.

There wasn't enough time for the stuff that really mattered because someone else's "urgent" needed my focus, energy, and attention NOW, while my own "important" had to wait until someday. Maybe you, like me, have always been the "responsible" one, the one who gets things done, who puts others first, rarely says No, and hates to disappoint or let anyone down? You probably already know that it's often the perfect recipe for exhaustion and overwhelm, while we wait for others to see the pressure, we're under or the stress that we're feeling. To be honest, I found it easier to get the job done, than to ask for help. But it often meant I was regularly busy sorting other people's problems and not having time for myself! What I wanted most was to have time for the simple things that mattered to me (more time with family, less stress, more fun) and that I could live a life that had time to include me.

The heartbreak of miscarriages.

I'd always assumed I'd have three children – you know the way we sometimes imagine our future when we're young. But my career took my attention for many years, and I was thirty-five when I had

183

our daughter Megan. As a nurse, I was familiar with the term "elderly primigravida" but was still a bit miffed when I saw it written on my charts in the hospital. I knew I couldn't wait too long to try to get pregnant again, but postnatal depression took its toll and getting pregnant again wasn't something I could consider for a while.

At 37, we decided to give it another go but over the following 3 years, hope became heartache again and again as miscarriage after miscarriage were part of our lives. After my first miscarriage, I remember being told by a friend that "I was lucky" because "at least it was very early in the pregnancy". I know she meant well but there's an aching loneliness when secrecy must be added to pain and tears to avoid insensitive (even if well meant) comments.

Supplements, tonics, and several frustratingly "normal" blood tests later, no one seemed to know what was wrong. We started that heart-wrenching journey into fertility treatment – if you've been there, you know the costs – financially, emotionally and on your relationship. That's a whole other story but take my word for it, it is not any fun! My nursing background made me wonder if I was in early menopause (because of the symptoms I was having), but I was told again and again that I was too young to be in menopause and that maybe I just needed antidepressants.

I'd used antidepressants when I had postnatal depression and I worked for a pharmaceutical company so I knew how valuable they could be, but I knew I wasn't depressed and that something physical was going on. But because I was the responsible type, I just kept going and no one knew how tough it was, how alone I felt, and how deep discontent had become my constant companion.

What really matters.

I'd always been interested in personal development and human behaviour and had read books on the subject since my early twenties (this was pre-internet times!). As my discontent grew, I read more and more, especially about how important our values are for a contented life. I became more interested in discovering my values in a practical, real-life type of way. I soon realized that I wanted to be authentic, curious, and brave in how I lived my every day. I knew that my relationships were jugular and that I wanted deep connections with the people that really mattered to me. But my work life balance meant I was compromising these values almost every day. I was also interested in a more holistic approach to health, but I was working in conventional medicine which rarely looks at the whole person or considers how one aspect of ill-health (e.g. stress or anxiety) can affect another aspect of the body (sleep, mood, motivation). I said my family mattered but they only got what was left of me at the end of long, busy, draining days. I knew how important time for connection, fun and play was with my daughter and that time passes quickly, especially when children are young, but time was regularly in short supply. I regularly joked that I'd "do

185

time for" the people that really mattered to me but all I wanted was to spend more time with them.

Dreams or Delusions?

What are values anyway? And do they matter in a busy life when you're doing your best to keep the show on the road? As a very practical and down-to-earth person, I wondered if values could be more than fluffy daydreams in a world that needed me to work to afford to live, never mind play? During my research on the topic, I came across a valuable resource.

The VIA Institute on Character (www.viacharacter.org). It has a simple, free, 10-minute scientific survey of character strengths to help you discover your greatest strengths. Research shows that knowing and using your character strengths can help you increase your happiness and well-being, find purpose and meaning, manage stress, improve health, strengthen relationships, and achieve your goals. Not bad for a free survey! This simple survey helped me realize my strengths and how I could begin to bring them into my everyday life. It also helped me learn more about human behaviour, especially my own, and how making simple changes can make massive differences to both calm and contentment levels.

There are thousands of books out there about values – what they are, what they mean, how you can identify yours, how to live a values-aligned life etc. and it's worthwhile learning more about the topic if you're curious. My pared-back route to finding out your values is to ask yourself three questions. Write down the answers to these three questions and let them percolate for a while.

On your deathbed:
What people / activities / stuff will you be happy you spent time on during your life?

_____

_____

_____

_____

What will you wish you'd done more of during your lifetime?

_____

_____

_____

_____

What will you wish you'd spent less time doing?

_____

_____

_____

_____

It's important to understand that most of us will need to spend some part of our lives doing stuff (tasks, jobs or maybe even our entire work life) that pays the bills and allows us to be contributing members of society. However, we need to ensure that we aren't using the remaining time on activities that don't align with or support our values. For example,

- How many of us say we value health but yet, we eat processed food, do very little exercise, and procrastinate about getting our bloods checked?

- Perhaps we say we value community but don't get involved or help with any local community-based events or activities?

There's a lot more to the topic of values, but the three questions above cut out the BS and are a great place to start for sure! You see, none of us are getting out of here alive and whether we like it or not, there's an end-date for each of us ahead. The pragmatist in me sees how useful it is to at least peek at my life and see if I can reduce the regrets list a little before it's too late.

Now before you think I'm going to share a lovely, heart-warming story about how easy it was to simply ask these questions and then make some changes, you're reading the wrong chapter! Let me first tell you about how life throws curveballs and how we often repeat the same mistakes again and again.

Hormone Hell and Martyr Mammy

I mentioned I'd had multiple miscarriages and had a suspicion that I might be in early menopause. Conventional medicine was no help at all – this was at a time when HRT was seen as the enemy and there was little information about the far-reaching effects those changing hormones could have on the body.

I was permanently tired and had aches and pains all over. My sleep was disturbed by night sweats, and I woke up more tired than when I went to bed. I lost interest in exercise and my social life because my motivation was at an all-time low. Desperation led me to do my own research, which meant I found the best solutions to get me through those few years but there were some rough times when it was hard just to make it through the day. With low energy often comes low motivation and before long I began to hear myself moaning, out loud and inside my own head. I was experiencing what I later described as *Martyr Mode,* (the belief that to be a good mother, I had to sacrifice everything for family and would feel guilty whenever I took time for myself).

"Can they not see that I need help?"
"If I don't do it, who will?"
"I wish they'd see how much I'm doing."
"Why doesn't he help out more or tell me to sit down to have a cup of tea?"

But the sacrifices began to feel harder as I felt sorrier for myself about "all I had to do". Resentment and disappointment began to build and I started to sound like my mother, even though I swore I never would. I was firmly in Martyr Mode and felt very powerless for quite a while. I sighed a lot and felt hard done by because life just wasn't fair. And the more "put-upon" I felt like, the less I took my own power. I'd promise myself I'd go out for a walk but get distracted by housework instead. Then I'd be cross with everyone because somehow it was their fault, I didn't get my exercise because they'd left the place in a mess. I'd wait for others to see what needed to be done (they rarely did) instead of simply asking clearly for help around the house. Then I'd be justified in getting angry because it "meant" that no one really cared. And I'd wonder if they'd even notice if I simply ran away. Oh yes, I was a barrel of laughs at that time, but I know I'm not the only one who's been in Martyr Mode because I hear about it from clients every single day.

I became a helicopter parent, which meant hovering around – just in case I was needed. It felt like I was always on duty, hypervigilant in case anything was wrong. I'd get my daughter into bed and then I'd stay up late – just to have some time for myself but would end up eating rubbish or drinking wine in front of the TV when an early night was what I really needed. No one likes a Martyr Mammy, not even the mammy herself. Let's face it, she's a bit of a whiner and she's certainly not living the life! But it felt hard to drag myself out of it – it was as though this was who I'd become. Does any of this

190

sound familiar? Have you ever been in Martyr mode? Maybe that's how you are now? You don't need me to tell you it's not fun and certainly doesn't help you live a life that makes your heart sing!

Mean-Girl Mode

Hormones are incredible and influence so much of our lives. In my natural health clinic, I help men and women understand the impact of changing hormones on their bodies and their mind. Hormonal changes in each decade will have a different effect on energy or mood and symptoms related to PMS or perimenopause can really take their toll. Premenstrual irritability can become everyday grumpiness and before long, your partner's breathing or chewing is enough to drive you wild. No? Maybe it was just me then?

We can joke about it and poke fun, except it's not funny when you're tetchy and lashing out at home. Maybe you hear yourself grumbling and finding fault with everyone and everything. Some days, you're so angry inside and everyone gets on your nerves but you're not sure why. Then, you're finding fault with your partner, and you wonder if they still care. And you're nagging your teenager about their room but actually, you're worried because they've been quiet and withdrawn. Yet, you'll still have that stupid row. And then after the outburst when you lose your sh*t in front of them all, you feel guilty and wish you could take back the mean words because they're not really what you meant to say.

Missing MOJO*

Did you ever catch a glimpse of yourself in the mirror when you look at your reflection as if to say, "What the hell happened to the person I once knew?", "When did feisty become flat?", "How did bubbly become boring?", "When did the lightness get lost?", "What do I even want anymore?" You're NOT alone.

Every day in my work as a Hormone Health and Mind Coach, I meet men and women who give their ALL to their family, work, and friends but who know that this way isn't working, but they don't know what to do. They used to be able to take on the world but these days, it's tough to drag themselves through the day. They've tried harder and given more and there's nothing left to give. Family means everything but low reserves mean they're distracted or drained at home. But they feel guilty when they do things for themselves – it's a no-win situation.

These men and women find it hard to take time for themselves because of the family, friends and work colleagues that lean on them every day. And because they're the dependable type, they're who others go to, so no one seems to see that they themselves are running on empty or low. This makes it tough to ask for help or to take a break and they wish they could wave a magic wand and remember the way to feel strong and in charge again. Hope can sometimes be low.

What is this MOJO*?

You, but on a good day, like you've been before.

Imagine feeling like yourself again – with the spark, drive, and energy you know and love. So that you feel like you can take on the world again and have fun doing it too. There's time for family, for friends and for you. You feel deep contentment again now that there's time for the important things in life – your family, your relationships, and your dreams.

Being on top of things again means you have time and energy for a life outside of work and you feel optimistic and hopeful about the future again. Your head is filled with ideas and your heart has hope again. You can hear your inner voice again – the one that's encouraging and kind. And the mean internal critic seems to have been dialed down.

Family is everything to you, and now you have the bandwidth and the headspace to be truly present with the people you love, the people you'd 'do time for'. Your drive, energy and motivation are back, and you can imagine a life that includes You. Because you know that's surely not too big a wish: *To live a life that makes your heart sing!*

As I said earlier, none of us are getting out of here alive and although getting older might be tough at times, it's better than the alternative for sure! My version of MOJO* is:

M – Motivation: to deliver on your promises to yourself

O – Optimism: about your future

J – Joy: simple joy and deep contentment in your every day

O – Original You: the fabulous, fun-loving, YOU that's been waiting for your permission to return.

Slip-ups and Self-Sabotage

Humans are incredible, and we sometimes do the strangest things. Have you ever noticed that we often don't do the stuff we know works for us or else we engage in behaviours that get in our own way? We know we feel better after we've been for our morning walk, but we get distracted with emptying the dishwasher or we start the online grocery order and then "suddenly", it's too late to go for the walk. Or we know that it's best if we don't keep sugary snacks in the house while we are trying to lose weight, but we keep snacks 'for the children' nearby.

I've loved watching people since I was a child. In my work as a mind coach, noticing human behaviour is a key part of my job. Because our self-sabotage behaviours are often hidden from ourselves, and we can only interrupt them when we have awareness that they're there. Isn't it amazing how easy other people's problems seem? If only, they'd stop doing this or start doing that – you don't see why they make such a big deal about it. Yet, clearly, it's more complicated than that because otherwise we'd be perfect ourselves. Being able to laugh at myself has helped me a lot over the years when I see the obvious in others and ignore the blind spots in myself.

Let me ask you two questions:

- What situations are likely to result in a slip-up in your self-care habits in the coming few months?
- How will you self-sabotage in those situations?

Remarkably, most of us can predict the answers to these two questions very accurately. Why? Because we usually slip up in the same ways on a regular basis. The good news is that knowing this makes it easier to intervene and interrupt those behaviours.

Situational Slip-Ups

One of the biggest reasons that people slip up these days is because life is busy! You probably hear people say: "The year is flying by" or "Where has the time gone?" Life, for many of us, is busier than before. The pace has quickened due to modern demands, both at work and at home. In the work setting, there seems to be more pressure - to finish tasks within tighter deadlines or get more done before the close of your working day. At home, after school activities mean every evening is filled with drop offs and catch ups and the family meal is often hurried, with little time for chat. The benefits of hybrid working can leave us with blurred boundaries between work and home life. It's so easy to check in on emails from in front of the TV at night and then wonder why when we go to bed we're thinking about work.

Self-Sabotage

Does a fish know it's in water? Mmm, that's a strange question for sure. But sometimes, our self-sabotage behaviour can be practically invisible to ourselves – as invisible as the water is to the fish. Take a look at the two self-sabotage behaviours below and see if either are familiar to you:

1. The Responsible One

You're the person who gets things done. You do a good job of keeping the 'show on the road' and to everyone else, it looks like you have your sh*t together all the time. And you do for the most part, except when you don't. Because sometimes your boundaries are poor and you say Yes, when you wish you'd said NO. And because you hate to let others down, you'll sometimes agree to take on more than you can realistically do and so, you end up sacrificing your time, energy, and headspace to deliver as agreed on time. And it's your own downtime that gets postponed, leaving you little space for idleness, connection, and fun.

It would rarely dawn on you to ask for help or an extended deadline – you simply cancel your own plans, feeling frustrated and angry that you've found yourself in this situation again. And your mean, internal critic will remind you of how you should really know better by now. Because being mean to yourself clearly helps here – in no friggin' way at all! But you can get caught in that combination of frustration and shame, which leaves you exhausted at the end of the day. It's worth remembering that self-compassion helps (not to be confused with self-pity).

2. The Procrastinator

You're the person who assumes there'll be time someday once you've finished everything on your To-Do list. Did you know that the likelihood is that most of us will die with an unfinished To-Do list? Yup, that caught your attention, didn't it? Which makes postponing your plans, your self-care, your dreams until all the jobs are done a high-risk strategy. I like to remind myself often that none of us are getting out of here alive – make sure you don't miss life for checklists!

Sometimes, however, procrastination is because it's scary or uncomfortable to look at what you want from life. You're afraid that you'll never know your purpose and what it is that brings you real joy, so you keep postponing until "things get easier" or "when the kids are finished school". Some questions worth asking if this is you include:

- What am I scared of?
- What do I think might happen?
- What am I trying to avoid feeling?
- Is it that I'm worried in case I get things wrong?

Humans are clever and the reality is that sometimes, it makes sense to put things off till later. However, if that becomes our default strategy, it may not be wise. Especially if you'd like to live a life that makes your heart sing.

Slow learners rock

I'm a slow learner (#slowlearnersrock). Some people seem to need only a nudge from the universe and they change their lives around. I'm the repeatedly-rolled-over-by-heavy-machinery-and-then-I'll -get-it' type of person. I could give myself a hard time about it but instead, I see it as the very reason I'm able to help others like me.

The fact that you're still reading at this stage in the chapter, I reckon that some of what I'm saying makes sense to you. Maybe you feel like 'I get you' or that my story resonates with you. In my work, I tend to attract a certain type of client. They're often in a professional role, perhaps a teacher, business owner or in a management or leadership role in their organization. They get stuff done, which is the very thing that has led to their success but it's also the trait that tends to unravel things for them too. But they're smart and decisive. And once given the support and shown the ropes, these men and women bring about change fast. Because life is busy, they like an approach that's kept simple and uncomplicated.

Deciding or Dithering.

Decision-making is a superpower – genuinely. If you think I'm exaggerating, take a look back at the turning points in your life – there was a decision involved in every single one of them. The quality of our decisions help us in a million different ways every day, from the simple: "What will I cook for dinner?" to "Will I go for the promotion?"

Clean decision making (my term) is when we assess the data, consider the options, check in with our own values, decide the next step, and then follow through with action. When we decide cleanly, it feels steady or solid in our bodies, even though we might also feel scared. A 'clean' decision doesn't mean we know the outcome or can predict the future - it means we are clear that this course of action is a good fit for us where we are today. We might still be scared or unsure of the outcome but we commit to the next step based on our values, not our fears. When we pay attention to our own internal dialogue in these situations, we notice it has a particular tone that's clear and at ease.

Dithering, on the other hand, is much less sure. We hesitate, change our minds, or want to know the future outcome before committing to a plan. We can feel it in our bodies – an unsettled or uneasy feeling. And our internal dialogue is often going crazy, with all the scenarios of "what-ifs' that it can find. Think of the times you've decided, rather than dithered:

- To say No
- To ask for help
- To get help with your hormones
- To hire a cleaner to help you at home.
- To say No to the soccer run or to be on that committee.
- To want more
- To tolerate less
- To start over
- To stop drinking
- To be kind inside your own head
- To stop playing small at work
- To stop whinging
- To be your own best friend

Why your decisions matter - the legacy you're leaving

It's often said that the wisest people are those who can look out into the future and ask how they want to be out there. As you look out into your future, how do you want to be? Five years from now? Or maybe ten years or more? What legacy would you like to leave? What legacy do your current behaviours mean you'll leave?

Every one of us leaves a legacy when we die; how we are remembered and the impact we've had on the people in our world.

- How do you want to be seen and remembered - by your family and your friends?
- What words would you like others to use to describe you?
- What impact do you want to have? On your world, be that your family, your children, your workplace, on your community, or on the strangers you've met along the way.

Decisions that Matter

Question: How do you eat an elephant?

Answer: One bite at a time.

Before you go into overdrive about all the decisions that need to be made, let me first remind you to take things one step at a time. When you're living a life that makes your heart sing, the decisions keep on coming. It's an ongoing process that continues while you're alive and growing. Living a values-aligned life means there will always be decisions to make as you move through the lifelong process of becoming who you want to be in the world. Here are some steps that may help you navigate your way:

1. Do the character traits survey to identify your strengths.
2. Use the results to inform your goals, your habits, and your hobbies.
3. Ask yourself about the legacy you want to leave in the world.
4. Begin to make changes with clean decisions.

A Life that Makes Your Heart Sing

The people, places or things that make your heart sing may be very different to someone else. Therefore, it makes sense to consider what a contented life means to you now. It also makes sense to check in with yourself on an ongoing basis. Because as you get older, your preferences might need to be updated and improved. Regardless of your age and stage, it's good to stop and check in with what a contented life (one that makes your heart sing) looks like. Here's my current description as an example:

A contented life has:
- *Time for what matters every single day.*
- *Deep connections with the people I'd 'do time for'.*
- *A set of rules that rock my world, not wreck my head.*
- *Hope for the future, for myself and the world at large.*
- *Clashing colours because who doesn't love pink and orange together?*
- *The 'knowing' that people are amazing – that includes you and me.*
- *An awareness that life is precious and brief and is not to be spared or saved till someday.*
- *An unfinished To-Do list.*
- *Brave decisions and follow-through even when I am scared.*
- *The wisdom that "someday" is always in the future and never guaranteed.*

A stitch in time

Have you ever wished that family members would tell you when the cornflakes were running low? Instead of waiting until they're gone? It's the same with the loo rolls and the milk and if you're the person responsible for getting food into your cupboards, you know what I mean! Just like adding things to our grocery list before we run out, it makes sense to intervene before problems take hold. Rather than waiting for issues to grow bigger, will you take a few minutes to check in regularly on the following:

- Your own health. When's the last time you checked in with your body and mind?
- Your own self-care. Is it consistent and nourishing?
- Your close relationships. Are they in good shape or do they need a little TLC?
- Your family of origin. Are they influencing your life more than you'd like?
- Your work. Does it satisfy the needs you have /expect from it?
- Your purpose. How content are you with the attention this gets in your life?

The 'What-ifs and the If-onlys'

"The tragedy of life isn't that it ends so soon, but that we wait so long to begin it" — Anon

Have you ever noticed how quickly time flies? One minute it's January or your children are starting school and the next moment,

203

you've arrived at year-end or you're helping them with their college choices. And none of us want the 'what-ifs' or the 'if-onlys':

- Growing apart from our partner because we don't really know them that well anymore.
- Wishing we'd hung out more with our children as we see them prepare to leave home.
- Realizing that we've neglected our health or our body because we were too busy at work.
- Losing connection with friends we used to love dearly but haven't met much in recent years.
- Seeing that we could have managed that promotion or thrived if we'd changed career.
- Finding out that you've spent years aimlessly being a 'service-provider' to others, without ever asking yourself what you really want from life.

A life that makes your heart sing will of course mean that you might, in hindsight, wish you'd done some things differently. But by checking in regularly to ensure that your life is aligned with your values, it makes it easier to avoid the 'what-ifs' and the if-onlys'.

A life that makes your heart sing

Life is pretty spectacular, in both the most incredible and in tough ways. But none of us are getting out of here alive so it makes sense to me to find the easiest, loveliest, and most contented way of navigating our way through it. I hope the words I've shared here help you find your easiest, loveliest, and most contented way through so you can live a life that makes your heart sing.

Go gently,
Ashleigh Xxx

CHAPTER 12

A New Dawn - Let your light shine.

by Dawn Auchmuty

Over the years, having gone through many life events, I have come to realize that making effective and sound decisions is so important. It is an art that creates clarity, an art you can master over time, fine tune, and become really good at. The quality of your life is the living outcome of all your daily decisions, and your ability to make better decisions grows when you focus on the desired outcome or objective. If you look at the word itself and change it slightly it could be read as to *decide on* — the act or process of deciding.

I studied classical music in my younger years. I started out learning the basics and went on to read and play music to a high standard. It did not happen overnight; it was a 10-year journey. I could say the beginning was not overly exciting, I was not playing complex pieces, but over time with consistent effort and the decision to practice, I improved my skills. It started with a simple decision — I wanted to learn how to play the piano — and it grew from there. If I gave up in the earlier years, which I can tell you I felt like on many occasions, I would not have reached my final exam, grade 8, which is the highest grade you can reach in piano. If you take a moment to look back over your life and see what you have accomplished, you will see that you have made many good decisions that you should be so

206

proud of, especially during the times you did not give up. You stayed with it because something in you had a burning desire to reach the goal despite obstacles. It is often easy to forget the journey once you make a decision, but the journey is part of it, and not just what you go through along the way but how amazing it is to look back and see the progress, all the effort and time given.

What if you took a moment to pause and think about the impact one decision makes, one positive action can propel you towards reaching your dreams and goals. If one decision can do that then think about the impact continuous good decisions would have on your life and those around you.

Think of your life in the context of a beautiful masterpiece, a painting. Take a moment to visualize an expansive landscape. The sky, the terrain, the colours, the textures, the season, and all the details that you can see. Now think about the artist of this painting, you are the artist that gets to decide the scene that is unique to you. You see a finished image before it has even begun. Now the exciting task begins when you gather all the necessary tools needed, paint, brushes, clothes, canvas and an easel, perhaps even images of a scene you love to help inspire you on this journey. It starts with an idea, a vision that you see of a finished picture. Then the process begins, drawing the scene, blending paint, brush strokes, layering, creating. Without realizing you are making continuous decisions whilst painting, the colours and the tone, you become engrossed in this, and you know that with each step you are working towards a desired outcome.

Maybe during this creative process you make changes, you try something and find it's not working, so you find another way, but even if you make changes as you go along, you do not stop, you find momentum, and eventually what started out as a white canvas becomes a stunning painting. Have you ever been to an art exhibition, marveled at what you saw, taken time to take it all in, stood there in awe? How much more amazing is it to think that your life is so much more than a highly valued piece of art, your life is priceless. Your life is of high value, your dreams, desires, and goals are all relevant. Your legacy, the value of the life you are now living will carry on for generations, and just like a painting it tells a unique story.

Our choices impact not only us but those around us, just like the ripple effect of a stone in calm water, the circles move outwards. By making conscious decisions we can align our decisions with our values and our goals, embracing change to achieve our full potential. Your destiny is shaped by your choices not your circumstances. How you choose to live your life is the legacy that others will remember you by and the best way to leave a legacy that is worthy of your calling is to make the right decisions for you, your family, and your future.

Over 14 years ago whilst just having recovered from surgery, I was very frail. I had returned to work with many things on my mind, and I was vulnerable, scared, and daunted because I was facing a situation that was no longer serving my greatest good. I had been unhappy in my marriage for some time. My home environment was not peaceful, and it was impacting not only me but my children. It was a challenging time. It was a really difficult situation with a lot of conflict. At times it was hard to see the woods from the trees, to make sense of it all. So many emotions arose. It was overwhelming knowing that I may need to make some decisions for change but feeling too weak and not "ready" to make them.

Where do you go when life feels so fragmented? They say home is where the heart is, and my heart was broken. I was a shell of my former self. I felt like a shadow and not real, I just wanted to hide in a corner. I wanted to run but where would I go? I had 2 children that needed me, I had responsibilities, I had an extended family, I had a house to maintain. The list seemed endless of to dos. This was not the happy ever after I had envisaged when I walked down the aisle. My world was crumbling down around me. I was broken, hurting, and dying inside. I had tried all that I could to save things, to try to be the hero in the mess. I also knew that I needed to help myself and try and process many difficult emotions. If life was to feel good, decisions had to be made.

I attended therapy in the hope I may get some direction, and after some time I knew in my heart that things were not going to change, and I would have to make some difficult decisions. The question I asked myself many times was should I stay in the same situation, a situation that is not going to improve, or leave so that I could in time be at peace and create a better and happier future.

I felt trapped, as though I was lying on the floor of a prison cell, sad and stuck, in rags of a dress, unkempt, bruised, and barefoot, a barred window in the cell and a barred door. There was light streaming in, the sun was out, and I could hear children laughing in the distance, the sound of the ocean, birds flying past, the warmth of a sunny day. It felt like I was very close to the sea, to happiness, but in a prison at the same time. The door could be opened and railed back. I wanted to leave this small place for something far more expansive, but I was scared. I felt in my heart that this sad girl could be happier if she put one foot in front of the other to move towards opening that door and leaving. I also didn't quite know how to do that because I had become familiar with life as I knew it. It wasn't how I wanted to live but there I was. Something in me believed that if I was happier then not only me but my kids would experience a better life and future. I knew it had to start with me and my decisions.

Many years prior I asked my mother a question, "What makes a good marriage?" and her words ring true to this day. My mum

210

replied, "When the rose-tinted glasses come off, which they will, the foundation is a friendship, an understanding between each other, through thick and thin that you will support, understand and love one another. Love is so much more than a feeling. It is the anchor through the storms that holds you steadfast so that you don't lose your way." They were wise words to a teenage me at the time!

My late parents were so different, yet it worked. They understood each other. Was it perfect? No. It didn't need to be. They made it work and they did their best at that time, for which I'm grateful, because they stood by each other, they raised 3 children, and they were by my side through it all. I trusted them.

I wanted my children to grow up to reach their full potential. I wanted them to grow up in a loving, stable and supportive home where they could thrive and flourish. I believed in my heart that they deserved a better version of me, a me that wanted to embrace life fully, fearless, strong, empowered, courageous and brave. I wanted to lead by example. Deep down I felt if I could focus on something positive, a guiding light, then I could move towards the light. My faith carried me through those darkest of days. Knowing that I was not going to be facing this journey alone brought me comfort. I also had the support of a very loving family to which I am eternally grateful for, and my faith was the lighthouse in the midst of the storm that I felt I was in. We all need a lighthouse to help guide us through the darkest times, because it is during those times that we question ourselves most.

Question after question flooded my mind. *What would my life look like going forward. How would I manage financially? How would my kids be? What would life look like raising my kids at home on my own? What would my parents think? What would people say? How would I navigate communication with their father. How would I navigate it all?*

My confidence was underground, my self-worth even lower, it all felt like such a mess at the time. I had a gripping fear that I can only describe as I had hit rock bottom, I could not go any lower. It was no way to live. I had shut down. I was becoming something I wasn't in order to survive. I felt like a stunned rabbit in the headlights, frozen, *'Do I stay, do I go?'* That unknown was a scary place to be.

From the youngest age I grew up in a faith-filled home, and as a child I loved many of the parables, but one that resonated with me at this time was The Lions' Den, whereby a man named Daniel was cast into a den full of hungry lions, not exactly the best predicament to find yourself in!

A stone was brought and placed over the mouth of the den, and the king sealed it with his own signet ring and with the rings of his nobles, so that Daniel's situation might not be changed. Then the king returned to his palace and spent the night without eating and without any entertainment being brought to him. And he could not sleep. At the first light of dawn, the king got up and hurried to the lions' den. When he came near the den, he called to Daniel in an anguished voice, "Daniel, servant of the living God, has your God, whom you serve continually, been able to rescue you from the lions?" Daniel answered, "O king, live forever! My God sent his angel, and he shut the mouths of the lions. They have not hurt me, because I was found innocent in his sight. Nor have I ever done any wrong before you, O king." The king was overjoyed and gave orders to lift Daniel out of the den. And when Daniel was lifted from the den, no wound was found on him, because he had trusted in his God.

In my moments of utter brokenness and fear I found that trust in God. We all have different names for God, such as Power, Source, Universal energy etc. I heard that still small voice saying, "Dawn do not be afraid for I am with you, trust me, I will protect you and keep you safe. Do you trust in me?" I had to think about it. I sobbed and said to God, "This is horrible, nothing about this feels safe, I'm petrified." I was silent for a bit and then something stronger and so much bigger than me said, "Dawn, I'm throwing you a lifeline.' Think about it, 3 hungry lions and a lifeline, which would you choose? I choose the lifeline!

Looking back at the Lions' Den parable, for me it was not only about the voice of hope but trusting that inner knowing, intuition, that still small voice that was cheering me on. That voice that was ushering me to make a decision that would not only change my life but that of my children and their children's children.

The unknown, because it is unfamiliar, can feel overwhelming and daunting. For me it was a scary, 13 years of marriage and "what is next?" would replay in my mind. How would the landscape of my life look moving forward? How would I be okay for my kids when I felt so much turmoil?

Taking moments to pause and breathe throughout that time helped me to gain greater clarity. I believed in God, I had faith. The story of the Lions' Den showed Daniel that he was not alone, that he did not have to do it on his own. Was Daniel scared? I'm sure the sweat was pouring from him, but God was there through it all safeguarding him. I had to lean into that inner voice encouraging me along. I had to trust that no matter what and no matter how afraid I was, things would be okay. They might not look it now, or for some time, but over time they would.

I have come to understand that the smallest step is an act of faith, but a step that has great strength in it. Choosing to believe in something better, stepping out of the familiar and into the unknown changed my life for the better. I had become so stuck in my life and I wanted more than anything to feel joy again, to feel light and free. I wanted to love me again, the me I was before all the conflict.

214

I remember sitting with my sister one day and she knew I was struggling. She asked me a question, "Dawn, do you want to still be in the same place in 10 years, where nothing has changed, or do you want to make a choice for change and hope for a brighter future?" There was possibility in that question for me. An opportunity to create something better, something happier.

The power of asking the right question was a turning point for me. Focusing on the problems, which were very real, was not changing anything, but changing the perspective, looking at it with a different lens could. A telescope into the possibility of the future was a new way of looking at it all. The "what if" as opposed to "help I'm drowning" changed the outlook. Just like an artist with a painting, changing perspective can shed a whole new light on what's before you. I needed change and I needed to trust it, it was the only way to create a happier life for my children and I. I kept repeating to myself, like the Yazz 80s song played in my head, "the only way is up baby for you and me now." I had to trust my own intuition, and having trustworthy people around me was important at that time. During my marriage, I doubted my ability to trust myself or my ability to make good decisions. Years of conditioning, almost losing my voice, and not owning my emotions had left me struggling to trust people.

As I child I suppressed my inner voice from a very young age, this carried into my teenage years and for a very large part of my life. I perceived that it was wrong to speak up, that it might upset others.

I learned that it was more important for me to take care of other people's needs to the point that I self-abandoned that voice of the little girl with a concept that I didn't matter. Part of me disconnected from the true essence of who I was, and when facing difficult situations, I would bottle up my upset and try to ensure everyone else was happy. This resulted in low self-esteem, disordered eating and fear of being the real, authentic me. However, having the right people around me in my darkest moments allowed me to reconnect to my voice, and I started to trust myself a bit more. It was a sounding board for me to be able to talk it out in a safe space and process thoughts, feelings, and emotions without judgement. It also taught me the importance of knowing who to trust, when to talk and when to protect. Discernment was a journey for me over those years. Learning to take back my power, to place value on myself and to trust my inner voice. I often refer to my inner voice as "the still small voice".

When I take time each day to simply be still and listen, calming my mind, I gain clarity. Almost like the observer, Dawn stepping outside of herself and looking in from a different perspective. Listening to what is arising without judgement. Listening to what it is that I need. Leaning in to loving compassion and kindness. This changes perspective and gives space to nurture those inner callings.

I believe that our true inner voice represents the essence of our being. This reflects our values, passions and desires. It is an unwavering compass, guiding you towards your purpose and the fulfilment of your dreams. Staying true to ourselves even when it is tough. It is about placing value on who you are as a whole. Every part of you matters. If you neglect one part of your life, it will reflect over time physically, mentally, and emotionally.

It's about self-love and self-care, like when you have a newborn baby, all you want to do is to protect them and give them what they need to thrive. I remember holding my children for the first time as newborns. The overwhelming love, the joy. When they hand you your baby, the reality soon dawns that *'Wow my life as I know it has changed, I am responsible for this new life, how am I going to do this?'* Something instinctive kicks in, you find your way. An inner knowing takes over. An inner voice. My baby needs sleep, food, love, shelter, and protection. You become that as a parent to your child. How much more do we need to be that for ourselves? Trusting that inner voice. It will guide you along life's journey. Over the years of our lives, we become conditioned by our perceptions, inherited concepts by parents, peers, teachers, people of influence, etc. so trusting ourselves sometimes must be re-learned. I have found the best way to do this is to question thoughts often and allow space for your inner voice to answer. In particular, the questions, *'Is it true? Is it helpful?'*

What if you came to the realization that you are not your thoughts, self-limiting beliefs, or preconceived ideas? You are more than that.

And what if you realized that if you are none of these, you can live without constraints? You have the freedom to simply be you.

I had to challenge old patterns of thinking to realize that and so I could heal and transform my life. The old thoughts were holding me back, they were not the truth. They were not serving my greater good. I had to learn to trust myself, the stillness of my inner voice, and my intuition.

It was at that time that I discovered Yoga, a discipline that gave me the space I needed to practice daily stillness and reflection. Yoga has proved to be invaluable for my wellbeing, so much so that I have trained to be a yoga teacher. It helped me come home to myself, to heal, to find my voice and expression through movement. It helped me connect again. It created a safe space that I could heal. It taught me how to listen, to sit with the stuff, with life. It gently showed me that everything about me was significant and that I was not my past, stories, feelings, thoughts or self-limiting beliefs. I was not the years of conditioning or other people's limited view of me. I could simply just "be". What a relief it was to learn this new way of being! It was transformative. My life no longer needed to be lived in fear, in judgement, the harsh inner critic. I was enough just as I was at any given moment in time. I did not need to be anything else.

It is so easy to become conditioned to thinking and living a certain way. As children we are influenced by our parents, peers, teachers, even social media. Our environment can play a huge role in shaping our minds and the decisions we make. However, our environment may not have always been healthy and this poses a question that maybe your perceptions and patterns were not always for your greater good. We cannot change what we are not aware of, however, when we become curious and more aware we gain knowledge and then we have the power to challenge and to change.

Have you ever heard the saying, *"You can't teach an old dog new tricks."*? It's a saying I heard many times as a child. The older generation telling the younger ones that at this stage of our lives we are not going to change, we are set, stuck in our ways.

Change is a choice. Challenging old patterns takes courage. What if not everything you are doing is serving you? Maybe take a few moments to explore your patterns of thinking and see if there are areas you could release and let go of and lean into the idea that you could create more useful patterns, new ways and new habits to create a very different way of living life. An upgrade. Who does not like an upgrade in life?

Well, the truth is, some people don't and won't, but let that not deter you. Changing your thoughts and creating a new way of living life isn't something everyone will get excited about. It is human nature to prefer familiarity and sameness, so the idea of you upgrading may cause some people to become uncomfortable, not that they don't want good things for you, but because it means things might be different and most people don't like the unknown. So, see this as part of the process, and that's okay.

Over the years of my life to date, I have come to recognize that this is where you need to understand the importance of having healthy boundaries. It will help you protect and value yourself and help you live a happier life. It may be necessary with family, friends, work and the wider world but having healthy boundaries is essential for your wellbeing. I need them to project my time, energy and emotion.

Without healthy boundaries there is chaos. Nobody knows what is acceptable to you and what is not, so to create calm you need to communicate it clearly. I have come to understand that it is up to each one of us to enforce boundaries to create healthier relationships.

I struggled with boundaries from a young age. I was raised by two very loving parents. They were not perfect, and they did their best, but as I child I did not question boundaries (most children don't) I just trusted my parents. This formed a pattern whereby I didn't feel I could express my emotions and really be heard. This created unhealthy patterns which I believe led to me being around very controlling people who were very quick to give their opinion as to how I should be. I became a magnet for toxic type relationships. The empath in me wanted to try to keep others happy.

If I was to describe it using an analogy, it was if I left my front door open for anyone to come and go at any time of the day or night. It would not feel safe, and if I continued to leave my front door open, over time I might become accustomed to intruders and eventually let it become a dysfunctional way of living. Not an ideal way to live, letting people walk all over my home with no respect for my space and for what I need to thrive. Boundaries are essential. Without boundaries life is harder. Remember, "Keep your head, heels and standards high."

I understand that this may be easier said than done. As someone who has been through the tough stuff, I truly get it. I know that feeling of wanting to feel you have everything "ready" before you make changes or before you let go of things that don't serve your higher good. Afterall, it's easier to plod along with what you know life to be, even if you don't like it, but what exactly are you waiting for?

Being prepared for something feels nicer but is there such a thing as every being ready? Having to know exactly what you are going to be doing, planning it all out in advance, etc. gives a sense of confidence but are we ever fully ready for anything? Things don't always go to plan no matter how prepared we are. Sometimes you just have to listen to your inner voice and trust that it will all work out.

I remember as a child when studying classical music and piano. Before each exam the nerves would kick in, especially as the grades increased and it became harder. My mum would say to me, "Dawn don't worry, go in and do your best." So, I would do that, and I did well each time, despite concern and worry. I think it is a natural response to feel uncomfortable going into an exam and some feel it more than others. You worry about how it will all go and hope that you don't make any mistakes or leave things out but it's not about being perfect, it is about showing up as you are and giving it your best. Life is the same. We get better over time when we create good habits such as getting up on time, going to work on time, completing daily tasks. All these build confidence within our ability to succeed. If we feel confident in our own skin then no matter what we face, we will go through it and come out the other side because we have a track record of showing up not only for ourselves but others.

It is the foundation of living your life legacy that others will remember you by, and the best way to leave a legacy that is worthy of your calling is to make the right decision for you, your family and your future. Once you commit to standing firm on what is right for you, you win every time.

I can now look back and look at my life today and see how much more expansive it is. I am a different person as a result of the decisions that I have made along the way which have been to my greater good. My greatest investment has been in my children, who are both thriving and flourishing. I am so incredibly proud of them. They have grown up into outstanding young adults and are excelling at all that they are doing. I am continuing to make better decisions. I am excited about my future, which is a vast landscape of possibility and opportunity. I celebrate this journey and am truly grateful for all that I have been given. I believe when we show up as our authentic self and let our light shine, this world is a better place.

So, let me ask you this, are you living your best life? Are you fulfilled? Are you thriving? If you were to look at your life right now as it is, are there any areas that you feel you could improve and what decisions could you make to create change? It is completely natural to feel overwhelmed if you are facing something that is hard. I stand with you in this, I know firsthand how challenging and uncomfortable it can feel. If I didn't make the decisions I made all those years ago, I would not be living the life I am living now and I want to encourage you today to look at your life with a new perspective, with fresh eyes, take off the murky glasses and see clearly that you are worthy of living well, flourishing and thriving, not only for you, your family but a much wider circle. Be You. There is only one of you in existence and this world is a much brighter place for having you in it. Let your light shine!

CHAPTER 13

Decisions that Shaped a Future

by Pat Slattery

Welcome to a pivotal chapter in my journey. As you read my story, I hope it resonates with your own experiences and decisions. Remember that the journey of life is continuous and ever evolving. The decisions you make today will shape your tomorrow, just as mine have done for me. Embrace each decision with the understanding that it is a part of a larger tapestry of your life, one that is still being woven. In this chapter, I invite you to reflect on the impact of your own decisions and the growth that comes from them.

My story is but one example of how each decision can lead to new opportunities and personal development. Together, let us embrace the journey ahead, knowing that with each decision, we have the power to shape our future.

In this chapter, I will delve into the significant decisions I made throughout my life, the profound impact these choices had on my personal and professional growth, and the invaluable lessons I learned along the way.

My story begins in Limerick, where I grew up in a modest environment that laid the foundation for my character and aspirations. Each decision I made, from leaving school at a young age to taking on various jobs, played a crucial role in shaping the person I am today. Every choice I made carried its own set of challenges and rewards. Each decision, whether driven by necessity, ambition, or a desire for independence, contributed to my understanding of life and my ability to navigate its complexities. With each decision came a learning experience that helped me grow:

Resilience: The ability to withstand and bounce back from hardships.

Resourcefulness: Finding ways to make the most of limited resources.

Perseverance: Continuing to strive towards my goals despite obstacles.

I have immense gratitude for the lessons learned and the people who supported me along the way. Understanding the implications of my decisions has been crucial in my journey. It has allowed me to appreciate the significance of each step and recognize the cumulative impact of my choices on my life.

Through each phase of my journey, I have experienced significant personal growth. From the early days of working multiple jobs to establishing a reputation for reliability and effectiveness, each decision has shaped my character and prepared me for future challenges.

225

While this chapter captures key moments in my life, it is important to remember that my journey is far from over. Life continuously presents new decisions and challenges, each with the potential to impact our paths. This ongoing process of decision-making and growth is something we all share.

Humble beginnings

Born in Limerick in 1970, I entered a world far removed from the opportunities many take for granted today. The early years of my life were spent in a three-bedroom council house in Ballynanty, a modest yet vibrant community. By the time I was 10, we moved to a slightly larger house in Moyross, a neighbourhood notorious for its scarcity of opportunities and its hard knock reputation.

Growing up as the eleventh child in a blended family of 16, life was a constant battle for space, attention, and resources. My father, injured in an accident in 1962, relied on an invalidity pension that brought in £70 a week — barely enough to sustain us. I accompanied him weekly to collect this meagre sum, witnessing firsthand the challenges my parents faced in managing such a large household with limited means.

Despite these challenges, there were bright spots. Youth clubs, summer camps, and rugby became pivotal in my early development. These activities provided a structured environment and a sense of belonging that was crucial in Moyross. They taught me discipline, teamwork, and the value of staying engaged and off the streets. Through these clubs, I learned that survival in our tough neighbourhood required a blend of street smarts and resilience—a lesson that would serve me well throughout my life.

Lessons from My Parents

When reflecting on the person I have become and the journey I have undertaken, it is impossible to overlook the profound influence of my parents, especially my mother. Their lessons, taught not through grand speeches but through their everyday actions and decisions, have deeply shaped my outlook on life and my approach to challenges.

My Father's Silent Resilience

My father, a figure of quiet strength, faced immense adversity with remarkable stoicism. Despite suffering an injury that significantly impacted our family's financial stability, and the absence of a compensation claim that could have alleviated our strain, he never allowed despair to overshadow his presence. His resilience in the face of hardship was a silent yet powerful lesson in endurance. Watching him navigate life's challenges without complaint instilled in me a deep appreciation for perseverance and the strength to face my own battles with a similar resolve.

My Mother's Resourceful Strength

My mother, tasked with the herculean job of stretching our limited resources to cover the family's needs, exemplified resourcefulness and strength. Her ability to manage our household on a shoestring budget was nothing short of miraculous. She juggled various roles with grace and efficiency, demonstrating that even in the direst circumstances, one could find a way forward. Her actions taught me several invaluable lessons:

My mother instilled in me a profound sense of duty. She showed that taking care of one's responsibilities, no matter how challenging, is essential. Observing her tireless efforts, I learned the importance of hard work. She worked long hours, often sacrificing her own comfort to ensure that our family had what we needed. Despite the difficulties, my mother never lost hope. She believed that with enough effort and determination, there was always a way to overcome any obstacle.

The support of my parents extended beyond their everyday sacrifices. When I made the decision to leave home at 16, driven by a vague yet powerful urge to chase a dream, they could have easily held me back. Yet, they chose to let me go, allowing me the freedom to explore and grow. This decision was not an easy one, especially considering the emotional and practical implications. But their willingness to support my journey, despite the risks, was a testament to their belief in me and their commitment to my growth.

I will always be profoundly grateful for my parents' decisions and sacrifices. Their choice to allow me to step out into the world and become my own person was pivotal. They did not stop me; instead, they trusted me to find my path and supported me from afar. This freedom and trust were instrumental in shaping me into the man I am today. Their example continues to inspire me, reminding me that no matter the circumstances, there is always a way forward. Their unwavering support and the lessons they taught me have been, and always will be, my greatest assets. The lessons imparted by my parents have been the bedrock of my success. From my father's silent resilience, I learned the importance of inner strength and the power of enduring through tough times. From my mother's resourceful strength, I gained a relentless work ethic and the belief that no challenge is insurmountable. These lessons have been my guiding principles as I navigated the complexities of life and entrepreneurship.

These lessons from my parents are deeply embedded in my character and actions. Their resilience, resourcefulness, and unwavering support have been the foundation upon which I have built my life. As I continue my journey, I carry their teachings with me, eternally grateful for their guidance and the freedom they granted me to pursue my dreams. Their influence is a constant reminder that with hard work, determination, and a belief in oneself, anything is possible.

The Turning Point:

— Leaving School and Entering the Workforce at 14

At the tender age of 14, I faced a decision that would significantly shape the trajectory of my life—I chose to leave school and join the workforce. This decision was not made lightly, but it was driven by a combination of necessity, ambition, and a desire to forge my own path. Leaving school at such a young age was a momentous decision. For many, school is a time for learning, growth, and preparation for future careers. However, for me, the traditional path was not an option. Various factors influenced this decision:

1. Financial Necessity

There was a pressing need to contribute financially to my family. Staying in school would have delayed the possibility of earning an income, which was crucial at the time.

2. Desire for Independence

I felt a strong urge to gain independence and start shaping my future on my own terms. The prospect of working and earning my own money was appealing and empowering.

3. Immediate Impact

I believed that by entering the workforce early, I could make a tangible impact not only on my own life but also on my family's well-being.

With determination in my heart, I embarked on my first job at Cruises Hotel in Limerick. Initially hired as a dishwasher, I was ready

230

to immerse myself in the world of work, no matter how humble the beginnings. The role of a dishwasher was laborious and often overlooked, but I approached it with diligence and a strong work ethic. I understood that every job, no matter how menial, was an opportunity to learn and prove myself. Within just three days of starting, my efforts were recognized, and I was promoted to hall porter, or bell boy. This rapid promotion was more than just a change in duties. This was my first taste of success and recognition. It taught me several important lessons:

The promotion validated my belief that hard work and dedication do not go unnoticed. It reinforced the value of putting in effort and striving for excellence in every task. This early success fueled my ambition. It gave me a sense of pride and motivated me to aim higher. I realized that opportunities for advancement were within reach if I continued to work hard and stay committed. As a hall porter, I was exposed to new responsibilities and interactions. This role required different skills, including communication, customer service, and problem-solving, all of which were valuable for my personal and professional growth.

There is a much broader impact of the decision I made at this point in my life. Leaving school to enter the workforce at 14 was a turning point that set the foundation for my future endeavors. It was a decision that came with its own set of challenges, but it was also rich with learning experiences and opportunities for growth. From a young age, I learned the importance of hard work and perseverance. These early jobs were not just about earning money; they were about building character and resilience. My rapid promotion taught me to seize opportunities and make the most of them. This mindset stayed with me throughout my career, pushing me to continually seek out and capitalize on new chances for advancement.

The decision to leave school and work full-time shaped my outlook on life and my approach to challenges. It instilled in me a sense of responsibility and a drive to continually improve myself and my circumstances. Looking back, I am grateful for the decisions I made and the lessons I learned early in life. The choice to leave school and join the workforce was a bold one, but it was necessary and ultimately beneficial. It set me on a path of self-reliance, ambition, and continuous growth. It was a pivotal moment in my life. It was a decision driven by necessity, but it opened up a world of opportunities and learning experiences. The early recognition and promotion I received at Cruises Hotel fueled my ambition and taught me the value of hard work and perseverance. This journey, marked by its challenges and successes, laid the groundwork for my future achievements and the person I am today.

Becoming a Doorman:
— A Pivotal Decision in My Life
By the age of 15, my journey took another significant turn as I found myself working as a doorman at a nightclub in Limerick City. This

role, while unconventional for someone so young, became a pivotal part of my life, shaping my character and providing me with crucial skills that would serve me well in the future. Taking on the role of a doorman at such a young age was not a typical choice, but it was driven by several key factors. The need to support myself and contribute to my family's income was a primary driver. The nightclub industry was lucrative, offering better pay than many other jobs available to a teenager. Growing up in Moyross, I had already begun to develop a keen sense of awareness and the ability to handle difficult situations. These skills were well-suited to the responsibilities of a doorman. The job presented an opportunity to learn and grow in ways that traditional roles did not. It required a strong presence, quick thinking, and the ability to read and manage people—skills that were essential for personal and professional development.

The decision to become a doorman was not without its challenges. The nightclub environment was demanding and often unpredictable, testing my abilities and resilience in numerous ways. As a doorman, I frequently encountered difficult and sometimes dangerous situations. Managing conflicts, dealing with intoxicated patrons, and ensuring the safety of the nightclub required constant vigilance and decisiveness. These experiences were challenging, but they also taught me valuable lessons in conflict resolution and crisis management.

Being so young in a position of authority presented its own set of challenges. Gaining the respect of older colleagues and patrons was not always easy. I had to prove myself through consistent performance and reliability. Over time, my effectiveness and ability to manage the door earned me a reputation for reliability, leading to multiple job offers from other venues. The physical demands of the job were significant. Long hours, late nights, and the constant need to be alert took a toll. Additionally, the emotional stress of managing confrontations and maintaining order required resilience and a strong mental attitude.

Working in a nightclub environment exposed me to various legal and ethical challenges. Understanding the limits of my authority, maintaining professionalism, and adhering to the law were crucial aspects of the job. Navigating these complexities required maturity and sound judgment, which I had to develop quickly. Despite the difficulties, I made a conscious decision to push on. Several factors motivated me to persevere:

Building a Reputation
I recognized that building a strong reputation for reliability and effectiveness could open more opportunities. This understanding drove me to excel in my role, knowing that it could lead to better prospects in the future.

Skill Development

I saw every challenge as a learning opportunity. Each difficult situation was a chance to hone my skills, whether it was in conflict resolution, people management, or maintaining composure under pressure.

Financial Independence

The financial rewards of the job were significant. Earning a stable income at such a young age provided me with a sense of independence and the ability to support myself and my family.

Personal Growth
The role of a doorman helped me grow as an individual. It taught me resilience, discipline, and the importance of maintaining a calm and authoritative presence in challenging situations.

Looking back, I am grateful for the experiences and challenges I faced as a doorman. The decision to take on this role at 15 was a pivotal moment in my life. It not only provided me with the financial means to support myself but also played a crucial role in shaping my character and preparing me for future endeavors. It was a role that came with significant challenges but also offered immense rewards. The experiences I gained, the skills I developed, and the lessons I learned have been invaluable. Pushing on. despite the difficulties. taught me resilience and the importance of perseverance. This journey, marked by its ups and downs, has been instrumental in shaping the person I am today and continues to inspire me as I move forward in my life and career.

My Journey — From Home to the Unknown

At the tender age of 16, I made a decision that would shape the rest of my life. Leaving behind the comfort and familiarity of home, I set my sights on the city, driven by an inexplicable urge to chase a dream that, at the time, I couldn't fully articulate or comprehend. Leaving home at such a young age was both exhilarating and terrifying. I vividly remember the mix of emotions that surged through me as I packed my bags. There was the thrill of venturing into the unknown, the excitement of new possibilities, and the fear of stepping away from everything I had ever known. I was acutely aware that I was leaving behind my family, friends, and the community that had been my world. This wasn't just a physical move; it was a profound shift away from the safety net that had always been there for me.

Once in the city, reality hit hard. To survive, I held down five jobs simultaneously. Each day was a whirlwind of activity, from early mornings to late nights, with barely any time to catch my breath. The work was exhausting, and the challenges were relentless. But I was determined. I didn't know exactly what I was capable of achieving, but I knew that I was prepared to work hard — harder than I ever had before. The journey was an emotional rollercoaster. There were moments of doubt and fear, where the enormity of my

236

decision weighed heavily on my shoulders. I missed my family, my friends, and the sense of belonging that came with being part of a closeknit community. Amidst the uncertainty, there was also a sense of purpose. I was on a quest, fueled by the belief that my hard work would lead to something greater.

Through the long hours and countless jobs, I learned valuable lessons about resilience, perseverance, and the power of hard work. Each job taught me something new and pushed me to expand my limits. Whether it was working in a foundry, delivering newspapers, retail security or working as a doorman, I approached each task with the same level of dedication and commitment. I was determined to make the most of every opportunity, no matter how small or insignificant it seemed. Even though I didn't have a clear vision of my dream, I kept pushing forward. I was driven by an inner conviction that my efforts would eventually pay off. I discovered strengths I never knew I had and developed a work ethic that would become the foundation of my success. The dream I was chasing began to take shape through my experiences, and I realized that my true potential was far greater than I had ever imagined.

Looking back at this part of my journey, I again find myself filled with gratitude for the journey. Leaving home at 16 was a monumental decision, but it was the catalyst for my growth and transformation. The challenges I faced and the hard work I put in were all part of the process that led me to where I am today. I learned that success is not just about achieving a specific goal; it's about the journey, the lessons learned, and the personal growth that comes from pushing yourself beyond your limits. The path from a young doorman to a successful entrepreneur was paved with numerous strategic decisions and invaluable experiences. The connections I forged and the skills I developed as a doorman became the foundation for my first major entrepreneurial venture: a security business.

— From Doorman to Entrepreneur

Working as a doorman provided me with deep insights into security operations, crowd management, and human behaviour. These experiences were instrumental in shaping my understanding of the security industry and laid the groundwork for my transition into entrepreneurship. By the time I reached my twenties, I was ready to take a leap into the business world. The decision to start a security company was driven by several key factors:

Industry Knowledge

My extensive experience in managing nightclub security gave me a unique perspective on the needs and challenges of the industry.

Network of Connections

Over the years, I had built a network of contacts who trusted my abilities and were willing to support my venture.

Market Demand

There was a growing demand for reliable and effective security services, especially during large events and festivals.

Strategic Decisions and Growth

Building the business required strategic planning and a relentless drive to succeed. Some of the crucial decisions that contributed to the company's growth included:

Recruiting the Best Team

One of the most critical decisions was to surround myself with the best people. I sought out individuals who demonstrated loyalty, determination, and a strong work ethic. By carefully selecting team members who were not only skilled but also shared my vision and values, I ensured that the company had a solid foundation of dedicated professionals.

The success of the business was largely due to the loyalty and determination of my team. I fostered a work environment where employees felt valued and motivated to deliver their best. This loyalty was reciprocated through their commitment to the company, which played a significant role in our success.

As the business grew, I made strategic decisions to scale up operations. During festival weekends and major events, the number of staff employed swelled from the core 185 permanent employees to hundreds. This ability to rapidly scale up was crucial in meeting the demands of large-scale events and ensuring client satisfaction.

The company's reputation for reliability and effectiveness was a cornerstone of its success. By consistently delivering high-quality security services, we built a brand that clients could trust. This reputation led to numerous job offers from other venues and established the company as a leader in the industry. Running a successful security business was not without its challenges. From managing a large workforce to navigating the complexities of the industry, each obstacle required resilience and strategic problem-solving. Some of the key challenges included:

Workforce Management

Managing hundreds of employees, especially during peak times, required robust organizational skills and effective communication. Ensuring that everyone was well-coordinated and trained was essential to maintaining high standards of service.

Client Relations

Maintaining strong relationships with clients was critical. This involved understanding their unique needs, providing tailored security solutions, and consistently exceeding their expectations.

Adapting to Changes

The security industry is dynamic, with constantly evolving risks and regulations. Staying ahead of these changes and adapting our services accordingly was a continuous challenge that we successfully navigated.

Personal and Professional Growth

The journey of building a successful security business was characterized by intense hard work, strategic thinking, and a relentless drive to succeed. It was a period of immense personal and professional growth. Some of the key lessons learned included:

Leadership

Leading a large team taught me invaluable lessons in leadership. I learned the importance of clear communication, inspiring others, and leading by example.

Strategic Thinking

The ability to think strategically and plan for the long term was crucial. Every decision, from hiring to scaling operations, required careful consideration and foresight.

Resilience

The challenges faced along the way reinforced the importance of resilience. I learned to remain focused and determined, even in the face of adversity.

Looking back, I am deeply grateful for the experiences and the people who contributed to the success of the business. The loyalty and determination of my team, the trust of our clients, and the lessons learned from every challenge have been invaluable. The decision to start and build a security business was a pivotal moment in my entrepreneurial journey. It was a venture that required intense hard work, strategic decisions, and a relentless drive to succeed. The success of the business, turning over £25 million in its lifetime, stands as a testament to the power of determination, effective team-building, and strategic planning. This period of my life not only shaped my professional career but also taught me invaluable lessons that continue to guide me in all my endeavors. As I continue my journey, I remain committed to facing new challenges with the same resilience and strategic mindset that fueled my success in the security industry.

Success in the security business gave me the confidence and capital to diversify into other areas. Over the years, I have owned and managed several successful companies, including a waste management company, an online marketing firm, and various ventures in multilevel marketing and referral groups. Each business taught me something new about resilience, market trends, and the importance of adapting to change.

One of my more memorable ventures was owning an Irish pub in Lanzarote. This business was not just about profit; it was an adventure in cultural exchange and community building. Another interesting endeavor was launching a milkshake and smoothie business. This venture, although different from my previous businesses, allowed me to explore the food and beverage industry, teaching me valuable lessons about product development and customer service.

Mentorship and Personal Development

As my career progressed, I discovered a deeper passion: mentoring and personal development and the joy of making a difference. Helping others achieve their dreams and goals became a central theme in my life. Whether it was through formal mentorship programs, business consultations, or personal advice, I found immense satisfaction in guiding others. Several key figures have influenced this part of my journey. My mother, with her unwavering strength, remains my greatest inspiration. In business, mentors like Brian Tracy, author of numerous bestsellers on personal and professional growth, have shaped my thinking and approach. The late Donie O'Callaghan, a great friend and confidant, also played a significant role in my personal and professional development. Yet, the most consistent source of inspiration comes from the everyday people I meet—entrepreneurs and dreamers striving to make a difference in their lives.

Reflections and Advice

If I were to offer one piece of advice to aspiring entrepreneurs, it would be to remain patiently persistent. Patience and persistence are the cornerstones of entrepreneurial success. The journey of entrepreneurship is rarely smooth. Challenges and frustrations are inevitable, but patience and persistence are key. It often takes longer and costs more than initially expected to achieve success, but those who stay the course and learn from others' experiences usually find their way.

Patience is the ability to stay calm and maintain a long-term perspective amidst the inevitable delays and setbacks. For entrepreneurs, this means understanding that success is not an overnight phenomenon.

Long-term Vision

Individuals and entrepreneurs must keep their eyes on their long-term goals. This involves not getting discouraged by short-term failures and setbacks but viewing them as part of the larger journey toward success.

Steady Progress

Patience allows for the steady, consistent progress that is crucial in the early stages of a business. It helps entrepreneurs focus on building a strong foundation, which is essential for long-term stability and growth.

Resilience

Patience cultivates resilience. It teaches entrepreneurs to withstand the pressures and stresses of building a business. Those who are patient are better equipped to handle the ups and downs that come with entrepreneurial territory.

Persistence is the determination to keep pushing forward despite difficulties and repeated failures. It is the fuel that drives entrepreneurs to continue striving for their goals. Persistent entrepreneurs do not give up easily. They face obstacles head-on and find ways to overcome them. This tenacity is what often separates successful people from those who give up too soon.

Learning and Adaptation

Persistence involves a willingness to learn from mistakes and adapt strategies accordingly. Every setback is an opportunity to gain insights and improve. Persistent people continuously refine their approaches based on feedback and experiences.

Innovation and Creativity

Persistence fosters innovation and creativity. When initial attempts fail, persistent people explore alternative solutions and come up with innovative ideas to achieve their goals. This relentless pursuit of success often leads to groundbreaking innovations. The combination of patience and persistence creates a powerful mindset for individual people:

Balanced Approach

Patience ensures that people do not rush into decisions without adequate preparation, while persistence ensures that they do not abandon their goals at the first sign of difficulty. This balance is critical for sustainable growth.

Building Relationships

Building a successful business often involves creating strong relationships with customers, investors, and partners. Patience helps in nurturing these relationships over time, while persistence helps in maintaining and strengthening them, even when challenges arise.

Achieving Milestones

Those who are both patient and persistent are better equipped to achieve their milestones. They understand that each small achievement is a step towards their larger goal and remain committed to the process, regardless of the pace.

The journey of entrepreneurship is a marathon, not a sprint. Remaining patiently persistent will allow you to navigate the inevitable challenges and setbacks with a long-term perspective and unwavering determination. By embracing patience and persistence, it is highly likely that you will increase your chances of not only achieving your goals but also building a resilient and innovative business that stands the test of time.

Pride in My Sons

Among my greatest accomplishments are my 4 sons. Watching them grow into outstanding men fills me with immense pride. Their successes and the values they embody are a testament to the lessons and examples set by me, my wife, and my parents.

Continuing the Journey

Although I have achieved a great deal, I am far from done. At 53 years young, I feel I have another 50 years to give. My mission now is to continue making a difference in the lives of millions, providing hope and a sense of possibility to those who need it most.

Challenges and Triumphs - Overcoming Adversity

Life in Moyross was a crucible of adversity. The environment was tough, and opportunities were scarce. However, this adversity taught me invaluable lessons about resilience and resourcefulness. These qualities were crucial in overcoming the numerous challenges I faced in both my personal and professional life. Starting and running a successful business is never easy. There were times when I faced financial difficulties, market fluctuations, and intense competition. However, each challenge was met with determination and a willingness to adapt. This mindset was crucial in navigating the complex and often unpredictable world of business.

Learning from Failures

Not all my ventures were successful. There were failures and setbacks along the way. However, each failure was a learning opportunity, teaching me what not to do and how to improve. These lessons were invaluable in refining my strategies and approaches in subsequent ventures.

Giving Back

One of the most rewarding aspects of my journey has been mentoring future leaders. Sharing my experiences and insights with young entrepreneurs and business owners has been incredibly fulfilling. Seeing them succeed and knowing that I played a part in their journey is a source of great pride. Engaging with the community and giving back has always been important to me. Whether through formal programs or informal interactions, I strive to make a positive impact on the community that shaped me. This commitment to giving back is a central part of my legacy.

Looking Forward

As I look to the future, my goal is to expand my reach and impact. Through seminars, workshops, and personal mentorship, I aim to touch the lives of millions more. The world is full of potential, and I am committed to helping others realize theirs. The business world is constantly evolving, and I am excited about the new opportunities that lie ahead. Embracing change and staying ahead of the curve will be crucial in continuing my journey of success and impact

248

Continuing Personal Growth

Personal growth is a lifelong journey. I am committed to continuously learning and evolving, both as a person and as a professional. This commitment to growth is what drives me and keeps me motivated to achieve more. The story of my life is one of resilience, determination, and the relentless pursuit of success. From humble beginnings in Moyross to becoming a successful entrepreneur and mentor, each decision I made shaped my future in profound ways. The lessons I learned, the people I met, and the challenges I overcame have all contributed to the person I am today. As I continue my journey, my focus remains on making a difference, inspiring others, and achieving even greater success. My story is a testament to the power of determination, hard work, and the courage to step into the unknown. It's a reminder that even when the path ahead is unclear, taking bold steps and persevering through challenges can lead to extraordinary outcomes. So, to all the aspiring leaders out there, remember that your journey may be filled with uncertainty, but it's also brimming with potential. Embrace the fear, chase your dreams relentlessly, and never underestimate the power of your hard work and dedication. Decide what you want, create a plan, commit to your decision and take action!

HAVE AN OUTSTANDING DAY (I KNOW I WILL).

CHAPTER 14

The Power of Decision

by Shane Coyle

As I reflect on how and why my life has changed dramatically over the past few years, I think back to the days where I was aspiring to be a successful property investor and binging on the TV show 'Homes Under the Hammer'. I loved the thought of buying a smelly old house, fixing it up and selling it on for a substantial profit. I was so inspired by these investors that just swooped in there and picked up a bargain property at auction and then made a fortune on it after the renovation. The more I emersed myself in this TV show I could see how possible it was to make a living out of this if you just repeated the same process over and over again. My mind was made up, I was sold, I said to myself, "That will be me some day, I'm going to make this happen!"

So how did I get from binge watching a TV show to running an award-winning property investment business in the space of a few short years? Let me share the strategic methodology that I have applied and some of the core principles I've practiced along the way which will apply to any aspiring entrepreneur within any industry. I made the decision to implement the *Plan, Do, Check, Act* (PDCA) methodology. This methodology can be applied to any discipline, project, or big goal that you might have. I'm going to unpack this with you so you can be confident that you can implement it in your own life and business.

Let me take you on a journey where I discovered these key principles and how they helped turn my dream into a reality!

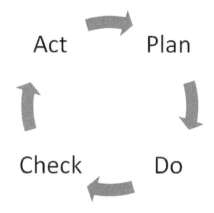

PLAN!

Establishing objectives and processes to achieve the desired results.

Principle 1 – Planning

When I think back to making the decision that I was going to become a successful property investor, one of the biggest mistakes I made was right at the beginning as I didn't really have a structured plan on how best to achieve this goal. I may have had "half a plan" buried in my head, but by no means was it structured in any way. Without having a clear path on where you are going, how are you supposed to find your way? This can be true for many things, but for investing your hard-earned cash into a portfolio of assets that could potentially change your life forever, you need to make sure there's a solid plan in place. By the way, that "hard earned cash" I'm referring to, I didn't have any of it at this point, but we'll get to that!

Let me give you an example of where NOT having a plan has impacted me on my journey so far. As I was saving up for my first investment property, I didn't have a plan to educate myself, no plan for what type of property I was going to buy, how much should I budget for? What would be considered a good investment property? I was so eager just to get going and I didn't have the patience to go about it in the right way. My thoughts at the time were "just give me any old thing and I'll figure it out!" Needless to say, this is not the most strategic way to be starting your journey for becoming a successful property investor.

When I made that first purchase, I did not finance it correctly, it was leaving me with barely anything to come and go on at the end of each month once all the expenses had been paid. I didn't buy the property in the right area where it had potential to greatly appreciate over time. I didn't know what my exit strategy was. Why was I buying this? How can I get the highest return out of this asset? What contingencies are in place if things don't go according to plan? I didn't account for any of these key factors in my decision making.

I'm a big advocate for a great book called *'Who Not How'* by Dan Sullivan and Benjamin Hardy. This book explores a formula on how to achieve bigger goals, not by knowing *how* but by knowing *who*. I can relate to this in many ways, which I will explain through the various principles we explore throughout this chapter. However, knowing how should not be dismissed as irrelevant, you must plan accordingly and at least document a roadmap on how you are going to get from A to B and some of the key milestones to aim for along the way.

Principle 2 – Education

I would imagine the first thing that comes to people's minds when they think of Education is what experiences they had in school. My memories of school days are of complete boredom, struggling to get through each day, constantly looking at the clock and wishing someone would teleport me out the door. I was not there because I wanted to learn, I was there because that's where society told me to be!

Looking back on my secondary school years, I often think, what was the point? I now run an award-winning property business, yet I despised my business studies class. I work with numbers every single day, yet I flunked every maths test I have ever taken. I'm now an author and a columnist for my local newspaper, yet my coursework from English class was never to be seen. How is this possible? It's possible because I had no passion for the generic, beige, out of date curriculum they are still teaching today. Thankfully I now look at education in a completely different way. This is because I now enjoy what I'm learning about, I can choose how to educate myself. I can research various educational opportunities that will help me grow and become a better version of myself each and every day. When you enjoy it, it no longer becomes a chore. If you have the right mindset that you are learning for the right reasons and it will add significant value throughout your professional development journey, I guarantee you this will be something you want to chase over and over again, especially once you start seeing the results from the effort you put in.

In terms of property education, if this is something of interest to you, my advice would be to approach with caution! Please be careful who you choose to educate yourself with, there are many "educators" out there and their only goal will be to try and line their pockets with as little effort as possible from their end. They will not live up to their promise on the course they are selling you, their priority will always be to make more sales. My advice here is to go deep on your research before choosing any coach or mentor, regardless of whatever industry you are passionate about. Try to get as many recommendations as you possibly can about their work, because once you find the right one it could change your life, forever. I am glad to say that I have now found a few mentors that have had this impact on me and will continue to do so for a long time to come. Be Cautious, Be Diligent, DO YOUR HOMEWORK!

Principle 3 – Networking

What comes to your mind when you think about networking? Personally, before I started my business my thoughts would have been along the lines of 'what a load of nonsense'. Networking is only for a bunch of brown noses trying to make a few sales. Now, this may be true in some cases, but boy do I need to eat my own words because over the past few years I have now learned that networking is without doubt one of the most important factors for taking your business to that next level. If you want to learn, grow and achieve your goals much quicker, so much of this will be dependent on the network you have built around you, especially if you are a sole trader, or a one-man band. If you try spinning too many plates and doing everything on your own, you will struggle!

Networking for me is not about making sales, it's about building relationships. The relationships may end up leading to sales, but the underlaying aspects of building a good solid relationship with people you get to know, like and trust will be worth its weight in gold. Find a networking community that is supportive, find a network that is welcoming, find a network that loves to hear about your wins and keeps you pushing forward. Support others, help people in your network in any way you can because one day they might just return that favour, or make that introduction, or give you that leg up when things are falling by the wayside.

Joining a networking community was in no way easy for me at the start, it took me quite some time to settle in and build up the courage to initiate a conversion with a total stranger. As an introvert, I always knew this was going to be challenge. But I was willing to give it a go, I knew that if I wanted to build a solid network around me then it was up to me and only me to put the effort in. No point waiting about for other people to approach me, take a deep breath, get rid of all those negative pointless thoughts that serve no purpose, eliminate doubt and just get on with it.

I now realize that networking is just like any other skill, it requires effort, it requires patience, it requires practice and eventually it will become easy, and you start to realize "what was all that fuss about?". I went from that shy little guy in the corner who wouldn't say boo to no one, to becoming a public speaker at various networking events throughout the country. Would I have gotten there without putting some effort in and continuously working on it? Absolutely not! It's a simple formula when you think about it, put in the work in, be consistent, reap the rewards!

DO!
Carrying out the objectives as planned.

Principle 4 – Discipline
I love this quote "Discipline is doing the things you hate to do but doing it like you love it" — *Mike Tyson.*

We must get comfortable with being uncomfortable! If you have big goals and big dreams this will require doing things that you don't want to do. It will require practice; it will require patience and it will most certainly require DISCIPLINE.

Don't feel like getting out of bed— get out of bed!
Don't feel like going to the gym— Go to the gym!
Don't feel like doing some work— Do some work!
Don't feel like doing something that makes you feel uncomfortable— Get comfortable with being uncomfortable!

Personally, I have always been very focused on having a consistent daily routine. I like to be punctual; I like to be organized and I like to know what priority tasks MUST get done each and every day to keep me pushing forward. Currently, the level of success of my business will be determined upon all of the choices that I make. If I want to make good choices, I MUST BE DISCIPLINED!

So how much discipline is required to achieve the success you desire? For some entrepreneurs it may require getting up at 4am, immersing themselves in cold water, followed by meditation, followed by gratitude journalling, followed by a list 10 other daily routines before they start getting some work done.-I like to keep it simple so that I can manage my time better. I'm a big believer in the power of a good morning routine to set you up for the day. For me it's going to the gym first thing, followed by a healthy breakfast, then start working through my daily tasks with a priority approach.

1. Most important tasks first, what tasks MUST get done today?
2. What tasks are important but can afford to wait?
3. What tasks are the least important and should only be done when all high priority tasks have been completed?

This is how I stay disciplined: I stick to a consistent daily routine and do everything that needs to get done with a priority-based approach. No excuses, just get it done!

Now we all know that life gets in the way. You might start your day with great intentions of getting everything that you set out to do done. For example, your car breaks down and needs to be taken to the mechanics, then you get an unexpected call to deal with an urgent family matter, then you need to run to the shops and stock up on supplies. All of this leaves you spinning out of control and you don't get one thing done that you had planned to do. How do you manage this? How can I be in 10 different places at the one time? What day is it? This leads me onto the next principle, mindset!

Principle 5 – Mindset

There can be a lot of pressure on business owners when they are the sole captain of the ship. It is their responsibility to steer the ship in the right direction and keep all those on board happy, content and most of all, safe!

Most people naturally are not cut out to handle this amount of responsibility and like any other skill, it requires practice. But how do you practice dealing with this amount of responsibility? I believe that a lot of this comes down to having a positive mindset, having confidence in your abilities and constantly working on your personal growth and development. Personally, I believe that working on your mindset is the most inspiring but also the most challenging skill to practice.

I'm a natural worrier, always have been. I spent many years in the corporate world assessing risk as part of my day job. My mind will usually automatically default to finding things that could go wrong, as opposed to what could go right. This can be a difficult setting to rewire and something that I continually work on. It's better to focus on the positives instead of the negatives if you want to achieve massive success. I would like to share a few things that I've learned as I continually practice removing the automatic negative thoughts.

- Say it out loud...
- Write it down...
- What is the likelihood of this actually happening?

If your brain is naturally wired to focus on the negatives, challenge them! Try and get some perspective for all these negative outcomes you are perceiving. Sometimes the negative thoughts you have are so far-fetched once you say it out loud you begin to realize how ridiculous it may seem. The same goes for writing it down, once you see it on paper you may determine that the likelihood of it actually happening is extremely low. Then you can start focusing on all the positive outcomes instead:

- What if this does work out?
- What if dreams do come true?
- What if one day I'm in a position where I've just realized "what was all that worrying about?"

Does this sound familiar? Think of the amount time and energy that goes into processing negative thoughts, why not put that same amount of energy into something more productive that benefits your business, your mood and all those around you that only want the best for you. Does this sound like a skill that's worth practicing? Absolutely! Having a positive mindset is key for any business owner. It can help them make the right decisions, keep their business pushing forward and most importantly, enjoying the process along the way! So, what needs to be done to continually work on your mindset? To focus on positive outcomes? To be the best version of yourself each and every day?

Firstly, get yourself into an environment where people support you, surround yourself with people who cheer for your wins, people who are genuinely interested in your mission and keeps you striving for success. Get yourself an accountability partner and keep each other accountable for your actions. This will help you both stay on track and focused on the tasks at hand.

Then you must avoid negativity at all reasonable costs! Do you really need to be watching the news every day to keep up with current affairs and be sucked back down into a fearful state of negative thoughts and worry? Ask yourself, how does that benefit you? What good can come from knowing all of the same awful stories, day in day out, that will only drag you down? Avoid negative people, people who hate to see others do well. You know the type, the type of person who is just waiting for you to fail so they can say "I told you so". Even though they never had the balls to try something new, something different and something that could potentially turn their life around with enough hard work and dedication. If they are happy staying in their comfort zone and judging others from a distance, let them be. Move on, keep pushing and keep your eyes on the prize. How sweet will it taste once they watch you succeed? mmmm yum yum!

Principle 6 - Taking Action

Hopefully at this point you have picked up a few valuable insights on how to take control of your business, how to set yourself up for success, how to apply various techniques to keep your mind sharp and focused on achieving your desired goals. None of this will be possible without actually putting the work in, taking massive action and doing whatever it takes to reach your destination. In this day and age there are so many distractions out there that may impact the level of success you are striving for. It is up to you to make good choices on what is most important to you. Is it spending several hours each day watching Netflix and scrolling through irrelevant garbage on your phone? Or is it time to start making changes? Is it time to start taking action and moving towards the perfect lifestyle you constantly dream of? What is your perfect lifestyle? Why is it worth putting the work in? You should continuously remind yourself of what this means to you. Why are you getting up every day and deciding to put the work in? Rather than wasting hours upon end being unproductive, de-motivated and getting nothing worthwhile done.

I regularly dream of this perfect lifestyle and how it would feel to start living that life one day. For me it involves more sunshine, more time at the beach, listening to the waves in a warm summer breeze, to have more time with loved ones whilst travelling the world and creating long lasting memories together. If I want to achieve this, I need to put the work in NOW to create a passive income and make all of this possible one day.

When will that day be? Unfortunately, there's no way we will ever know, but what I do know is that I'm going to do whatever it takes to make it happen. Put in the hard work now and reap the rewards down the line. We only get one chance at this life so why not go all in and give it our best shot? Not everyone will be willing to sacrifice the time now so that they can live their perfect life in the future, and that's ok. However, I am 100% ALL IN and thankfully I have a supportive team around me who understand that I'm a highly driven, motivated individual who has a very bright future ahead of them. Don't be afraid to say it, be confident in your words because one day soon your dream will become a reality. Remember, limit distractions, no complaining, no regrets... just get it done and one day soon the sun will shine brighter!

CHECK!

Evaluate the results to identify opportunities for improvement.

Principle 7 - Reflection

Do you ever feel like you are going 100mph every day and working from a never-ending To-Do list? Some days the list can be so long you think to yourself "Where do I even start?", "How am I going to get through it all?" In these moments of doubt and worry it's important to just step back, put the tools down and REFLECT on just how far you have come to get to this stage of your career. At times things can be moving so fast you forget to fully appreciate everything you have done to get your business to this level.

In the first few months of starting my business I was the master of going 100mph, BOOM! BOOM! BOOM! Moving from one task to the next, then on to the next, and I would then finally crash and burn at the end of each day because I was taking on so much. It was a great feeling to be able to get through all, but I was not taking that time to slow down, strategize and REFLECT on how each day went — *What did I learn from today? What went well? What could I have done better?* Thankfully, all of this started to change when I met a great mentor of mine, Pat Slattery. Pat helped me drive home the importance of reflection every single day. His advice is to capture all the things that brought you closer to your goal at the end of each day. To take that time and reflect on the positives, write it down, read it back to yourself, embed it into your head and constantly remind yourself of everything you are doing that is contributing to your success. It can be easy to forget this sometimes, it can be easy to get caught up in everything else that is going on and start to go off in different directions from what you initially had set out to do.

I was never one for writing things down until I met Pat, now I can truly see the value in taking just 5 to 10 minutes at the end of each day to analyse all the key factors that has contributed to your day. Then reflect on the positives, reflect on all the hard work you are putting in each day, reflect on just how far you have come and what motivates you to keep moving forward.

I would also recommend doing a much deeper reflection on your progress every couple of weeks. This will give you an opportunity to look at everything that has contributed to your wins on a much broader scale. Or perhaps everything you have been doing that has led to challenges, what was the source of the problems you faced?

264

What can you do differently next time to prevent it from happening again? This leads me onto my next principle...

ACT!

Taking action on the lessons learned

Principle 8 – Be Visionary

If you want to run a successful business, you have to be open to change and you have to be willing to make sacrifices and explore various opportunities with an open mind. If things are not going according to plan you need to step back, start looking at things in a creative way, be visionary and get back on track. There may be times when you are going off in different directions and you aren't even aware of it. This is why it's important to build a network of people you trust around you, people who will be honest with you if they pick up on something that's not right. My advice is to welcome the feedback from these people, be willing to hear their thoughts and make any changes you think might be necessary once you've had time to digest. However, please be careful receiving feedback from people who believe they know everything about everything. You know the type, right? They think they have it all figured out; they think they are the master of all trades. Please be careful of anyone like this that comes into your life and starts giving you advice about a business they know nothing about, this type of advice can be toxic! If taken seriously, it may lead to confusion, lack of confidence, lack of action and the worst all – FEAR! This is very common in the property industry. There are a lot of people that are very willing to share their views on where they see the property market going, people that will tell you that you're crazy getting involved in such a volatile market. Don't you know there is a financial crash right around the corner? Don't you know you will end up losing all your assets? Look what happened back in 2008, you must be MAD!

Whenever you hear this type of fearful feedback, regardless of the topic, just take a minute and remember all the hard work you have put in to get yourself to where you are today. Think back to all the hours you have spent educating yourself, the support network you have built around you, the resources you have available to you. Be confident in the choices that you have made, focus on progress not perfection, and consistently remind yourself of what your vision is. Where do you see for yourself in 5 years? Why did you start this business in the first place? What is your dream? What does life look like for you and those around you once you start to achieve those massive milestones along the way? Always remember your WHY, stay focused, keep going, apply each of these principles how you see fit and one day soon you will be the master of your own destiny.

I wish you all massive success on your journey!
Peace Out!

CONCLUDING CHAPTER

by Donna & Pat

The concept of "why" is the heartbeat of our actions, the silent force that shapes our lives and propels us forward. Understanding and embracing your "why" can be the catalyst for decision-making and the key to unlocking your true potential.

When we embark on any journey, whether personal or professional, it is the "why" that acts as our guiding star. It illuminates the path ahead, making our steps deliberate and meaningful. Without a clear "why," we are like ships adrift at sea, susceptible to the whims of the waves and the changing wind. Our "why" anchors us, providing stability and direction. And when we are anchored in our "why," we are better equipped to navigate life's fluctuations with grace and resilience. Our "why" becomes a source of inner strength, a reminder of what truly matters, and a guide through the uncertainty. It ignites us and it fuels us.

Consider a young artist, painting through the night. What drives them to create, to pour their soul onto the canvas, if not a deep-seated reason that goes beyond mere aesthetics? It is their "why" that fuels their passion, which compels them to express their innermost thoughts and emotions through their art. This sense of purpose infuses their work with authenticity and power, resonating with others in ways that go beyond the visual.

267

Similarly, in the realm of business, companies that thrive are those that understand their "why." Take, for example, the story of a small startup that disrupts an entire industry. It is not just their innovative product or service that sets them apart, but their clear understanding of why they exist. Their mission drives every decision, from product development to customer service, creating a cohesive and motivated team aligned with a common goal.

The importance of a "why" extends beyond individual and organizational success; it is integral to our mental and emotional well-being. When we are connected to our purpose, we experience a profound sense of fulfilment. This connection to our "why" provides resilience in the face of adversity, a beacon of hope during challenging times. It is what enables us to persevere when the going gets tough, to find strength in our convictions, and to keep moving forward despite setbacks and obstacles.

Imagine a teacher who wakes up every morning with a sense of mission. Their "why" is to inspire and educate the next generation, to ignite a love for learning in young minds. This sense of purpose infuses their teaching with passion and dedication, transforming the classroom into a vibrant space of exploration and growth. Even on the toughest days, when challenges seem insurmountable, their "why" keeps them grounded and motivated, knowing that their work has a profound impact on the lives of their students.

In our personal lives, the concept of "why" plays an equally important role. It guides our relationships, our choices, and our overall sense of happiness. When we understand why we are in a relationship, why we pursue certain hobbies, or why we make specific lifestyle choices, we are more likely to make decisions that cause us to lead lives that are aligned with our values and desires. Take, for instance, the simple act of exercising. For some, the motivation might be physical health, for others, it might be mental well-being, or perhaps a combination of both. Understanding the underlying "why" behind this habit makes it easier to stick to it, even on days when motivation wanes. It transforms the act from a mundane task into a meaningful routine decision that contributes to your overall purpose and well-being.

This was beautifully illustrated in the life of Viktor Frankl, a psychiatrist and Holocaust survivor, who chronicled his experiences in his seminal work, *Man's Search for Meaning.* Frankl observed that those who survived the horrors of the concentration camps were often those who had a deep sense of purpose, a reason to endure the suffering. Their "why" provided them with the mental and emotional fortitude to withstand the unimaginable. Frankl's insights underscore the profound impact that a clear sense of purpose can have on our ability to endure and thrive, even in the darkest of times. This was echoed when Donna interviewed Dr Edith Eger, also a Holocaust survivor. She put her decision to survive no matter what, down to having a why, a purpose greater than current circumstance.

In a world that can present difficulties and often emphasizes external achievements and material success, it is easy to lose sight of our "why." We get caught up in the hustle and bustle and things that, in the grander scheme of things, don't matter so much. True fulfilment and lasting success come from a deep connection to our inner purpose. It is this connection that brings joy, meaning, and a sense of accomplishment that transcends superficial measures.

Finding your "why" is not always an easy task. It requires introspection, honesty, and sometimes, a willingness to confront uncomfortable truths about yourself and your life. It is a journey of self-discovery that evolves over time, shaped by your experiences, values, and aspirations. But it is a journey worth undertaking, for the rewards are immeasurable.

One practical way to uncover your "why" is to reflect on moments when you felt connected, truly alive, and fulfilled. What were you doing? Who were you with? What aspects of those experiences resonated with you on a deep level? These moments often hold clues to your underlying purpose and passions. Journaling, meditation, and conversations with trusted friends or mentors can also facilitate this exploration, providing insights and perspectives that help you connect with your "why."

Once you have a clearer sense of your "why," it is important to integrate it into your daily life and let it guide your decisions, big and small. Whether you are choosing a career path, setting personal goals, or navigating relationships, let your "why" be the compass that directs your actions. This alignment between your inner purpose and your outer actions creates a harmonious and fulfilling life, where every step you take is infused with meaning and intention. a source of connection, building relationships that are based on shared purpose and mutual respect.

In the realm of leadership, the ability to communicate your "why" is especially crucial. Great leaders are those who inspire and motivate others by articulating a clear and compelling vision. They create a sense of purpose that resonates with their team, aligning everyone towards a common goal. This shared "why" fosters a strong sense of belonging and commitment, driving collective effort and innovation.

Consider someone who becomes passionate about raising awareness to address a pressing societal issue. The "why" is rooted in a deep desire to make a positive impact and effect change. By communicating this purpose effectively, they attract supporters, volunteers, and donors who share their vision. This collective energy and commitment amplify the impact of their efforts, creating a ripple effect that extends far beyond the individual. Ultimately, the power of a "why" lies in its ability to transform our lives from the inside out. It shifts our focus from external validation to internal fulfilment, from aimless activity to purposeful action. It is the foundation upon which we build our dreams and aspirations, the driving force that propels us towards our highest potential.

By embracing our "why," we unlock a source of motivation and resilience that empowers us to overcome challenges, seize opportunities, and live a life of meaning and purpose. Your "why" is the root of your decisions. Find your "why", find your why and fly. Change is not always easy It is not the smartest people that achieve success, it is the people that 'decide' to take actions everyday towards the goals that they want to achieve, especially when the going gets tough, especially when they feel like throwing in the towel

The one thing you cannot control in this world is events, however, you can choose what to focus on, what things mean. You can always make a decision, that is always in your control Staying in an unhappy environment is a decision. Giving up when the going gets tough is a decision. Allowing circumstance to determine your future is a decision. Staying with something that's not working is a decision.

"Indecision is the thief of opportunity" — *Jim Rohn*

Indecision means the opportunity waits, indecision means what could be is postponed and may never be. Never leave the sight of setting a goal without taking action, without doing something that commits you to the goal. If you don't move immediately on that thought, that action, that thing that you need to do, your brain is going to talk you out of it. If you don't decide to move very quickly from idea to action, your brain will sabotage you. Stop hitting the snooze button when it comes to making decisions, especially those that move you closer to your why. Allow yourself to believe that anything is possible, choose to be intentional and deliberate about whatever it is that you desire, choose to be intentional and deliberate with your decisions. All progress has been achieved because of decisions to be intentional and deliberate.

The Confucian saying, "A journey of a thousand leagues begins with a single step" simply means that great accomplishments begin with your willingness to face the inevitable uncertainty of any new enterprise and step out boldly in the direction of your goal. Choose to step in the direction of your goal. You can put off making a decision for a long time, but what does that really get you? It's just a stall tactic that buys very little and may cost a lot.

The wiser approach is to carefully review your options and single out the one that has the most positives going for it. Then, act. It's much better than sitting by the sidelines doing nothing. Avoid trying to second-guess yourself once you've carefully reviewed the options you have and chosen one to act upon. Second-guessing never produces optimum results but learning from your experiences does. If it doesn't work, do something else. No one is going to be successful in making the right decision every time. That's not how life works. But giving up when you encounter disappointment or failure isn't the way to get the most out of life. Deciding to do something else, however, is.

If you stumble the first time out, it doesn't mean you're awful at making choices. It does mean there's a lesson here you need to learn. Take ownership of the lesson and figure out a new approach. You want and need to amass a successful track record. This will occur the more you make decisions with the full input of logical analysis. And then DECIDE to carry out the actions you've determined are necessary.

Find your best time to think about your decisions. If you try to make a decision when you're stressed out, tired, hungry, angry or depressed, the decisions you make may not be well-informed. Instead, pick a time when you're well rested, full of energy and receptive to taking action. This may be early morning, a mid-afternoon break, or after you wind down at the end of the day. Whatever time works best for your decision-making process, when you feel you can objectively analyse the various choices and come to a reasonable, workable decision, Use that time to your advantage. The choices you make will reflect this proactive approach. Ask yourself, *Am I a renter or an owner?*

We care more for the things we own than for the things we rent because we don't have as much invested in things that are temporary, there's not as much at stake. Have you ever washed a rental car? Of course not.

When you own something—whether it's a car, a work assignment or a relationship—you make an investment, usually involving some degree of sacrifice. When you rent, you can walk away without losing anything. If you're really committed to achieving your goal, go all in. own your decisions. Decide what is best for you, take action on those decisions, NOW!

Difficult decisions

It's understandable to feel hesitant when faced with decisions that can significantly impact your life or business. Here are a few thoughts that might help:

Break it Down

Sometimes, decisions seem overwhelming when viewed as a whole. Break them down into smaller, manageable steps. This makes the process less intimidating and more achievable.

Visualize the Outcome

Envision the positive impact of making this decision. How will it benefit your life or business? Having a clear picture of the potential rewards can motivate action.

Set a Deadline

Procrastination often thrives in the absence of a deadline. Set a reasonable timeline to make the decision. Having a timeframe can create a sense of urgency.

Seek Advice

Talk to someone you trust or seek advice from someone experienced in that field. Sometimes, an outside perspective can provide valuable insights or alleviate concerns.

Accept Imperfection

Perfectionism can be a major roadblock. Understand that no decision is flawless. Aim for a good decision rather than a perfect one.

Focus on Progress Not Perfection

Recognize that progress, even if it's incremental, is better than no progress at all. Embrace the journey and learn along the way. Remember, making decisions, especially significant ones, often involves some level of uncertainty. But staying stagnant due to indecision might hinder progress. Taking a step forward, even if it feels uncomfortable, can lead to growth and positive change.

A final note that we would like to leave you with:

You Are Not Your Thoughts, however what you think about comes about! Choose to live in your new story! Choose to start at chapter one — right now! Practice the habit of making the best decisions.

What you can do

- Listen to your heart's intuition but pause before making any decision.
- Take time out and allow yourself to become relaxed and silent. Breathing slowly in the comfort of a relaxing space will help you do this. In the space of silence your heart and your head will consult with each other productively.

The following questions are great questions to ask:

- Do I feel good around this decision?
- Does this situation give me or take my energy?
- Do I feel empowered or disempowered?
- Am I going toward an adventure or running from fear?
- Am I listening to my lessons learned from the past?
- Would I make the same choice if I had a million Euros in my pocket now?
- Do I feel respected and valued?
- Am I trying to control the situation or am I leaving room for expansion?
- Will the choices I am considering bring me closer to that fulfilled life that I desire so much?

You are everything that is, your thoughts, your life, your dreams come true. You are everything you decide to be. You are as unlimited as the endless universe. Remind yourself - You didn't come this far just to come this far. We wish you a life of abundance!

Donna & Pat

THE AUTHORS

Donna Kennedy-Slattery

Donna Kennedy-Slattery (Psych (Hons), MGHC, MNLP) is a 7-times bestselling author, mentor, and highly sought-after professional speaker. She regularly features in media as an expert in personal development and her work has been endorsed by many well-known multi-nationals, including Google, Boston Scientific, AIB, and ENET. Her academic work has also been published by various faculties, including The American Journal of Psychology and The Irish Psychological Record. Donna has spoken at thousands of seminars, both nationally and internationally over the last 20 years, and her work has been referenced by global figures and used by leading organisations to train staff and accelerate growth. Her passion is to help people reach their potential and get impactful results fast. Through her in-person mentorship, coaching programs, digital products, and membership club, she has become known as the go-to authority in her industry.

"Donna's talk in Google was extremely well received. We found her content to be very strong!" - Google, European Head office

"Listen to this girl, she knows what she is talking about!" – Bob Proctor (teacher in the book/movie, The Secret

"Donna's techniques are powerfully simple to understand and use. You can unlock so much more inner potential and be far more successful in life when you control those inner demons inside your head." – Boston Scientific

"Donna is a caring, sincere and professional woman, a woman with a wealth of experience. This qualifies her to empower others to overcome all obstacles that stop them from reaching their own goals in life and above all to find real happiness and to love themselves." – Christina Noble OBE

"Donna has big goals and with her generous spirit she always includes everyone in them. Incredible speaker with amazing information!" – John Boyle, (founder of Boyle Sports)

Contact: www.donnakennedy.com

Pat Slattery

Pat Slattery is no ordinary speaker or coach. Leaving school at 14yrs old he began working in the hotel industry, and at 15 years old he began working in the security industry and over time built a company that generated over 25million Euro. He has an incredibly positive attitude and outstanding work ethic along with a determination to give 100% to everything he does.

Pat has delivered over 2500 keynote speeches during his 20+ years in the personal and professional development industry.

He has facilitated thousands of mastermind mentoring masterclasses that have helped thousands of individuals achieve their lifetime goals. Pats talks come straight from the heart, the ups and downs of business and life experiences, he gives practical information that he has applied himself that has driven him to the successes he has achieved in his life and business.

"Pat has one of the greatest minds in the world when it comes to personal and professional development." – Brian Tracy, author of 86 global bestselling books.

"Pats information is going to turn your economy right side up," Mark Victor Hansen (Co-author of Chicken Soup for the Soul)

"When it comes to change Pat really knows what he is talking about - because he has lived it, when it comes to managing change the man is a genius" Bob Proctor (The Secret)

Contact Pat: www.patslattery.com

Shaun McLaughlin

Shaun McLaughlin is the owner of Shaun Bill Coaching. A qualified personal trainer and running coach with over 18 years' experience. He has an extensive background in coaching, especially in athletics and running, with his athletes winning national titles in recent years under his direction. He specializes in endurance events but he is equally at home bringing someone along on their first 5k. From someone who "stumbled" into running just to keep a friend company, he went on to compete in over 45+ marathons around the world, is a multiple Ironman finisher and has completed numerous ultra distance events including the "Connemara 100" and the infamous 24 hour – 250km "The Race." Shaun, along with his partner Aileen, also an avid runner, lives in Donegal in the northwest of Ireland. A mechanical engineer by profession, he is also a firefighter with the Donegal Fire Service.

Contact: info@shaunbill.com

Facebook and Instagram: Shaun Bill Coaching

Maeve Kelly

Maeve Kelly was a successful Numerologist and Life Coach until a fateful day in 2016, when a man with a severe, unresolved mental illness hit her car head on with his own. This left Maeve with life-changing injuries. She was unable to work, debilitated, and in constant pain.

Since the accident, Maeve has campaigned for safer roads in Ireland and all across Europe, advocating at EU level to raise awareness. Mother to three children, Savannah, Casey and Abbey, and grandmother to Mia and Logan, Maeve invests her energy and joy into her expanding family. She also works part-time as a commercial model with Assets Modelling Agency and as an extra with Celtic Casting Agency and Movie extras. In spite of being quite shy and reserved, Maeve shines in front of the camera. She enjoys writing poetry and works tirelessly as an advocate for change and education in various charities and national networks. She strives each day not to let her experience define her but instead inspiring her into being a force of positive transformation.

Paula Esson

Paula is a spirited adventurer, who carves the path of life with resilience and fun. Bringing a vibrant spirit and active lifestyle to her exploration and discoveries. She bridges her days between Iceland, Northern Ireland and now Glasgow, creating opportunities for women to truly expand their capabilities and potential using the powerful force of nature and the land of Ice and Fire. Often creating limitless possibilities for those that join her and a true sense of personal achievement.

Behind the daring exterior lies a caring and compassionate soul, always ready to lend a helping hand to those in need and as a sport scientist she achieves this through hands on connection, a deep understanding of the body and the energetic link to the experience of pain to create relief and the path to your most creative life.

Her journey so far is a testament to the fusion of adventure and empathy, developing strength and balance for people who want to conquer challenges and do so with a heart full of compassion, friendship, and warmth.

Paula has really created, moved mountains and approached life with a steady resolve, however, she has always stayed grounded in the literal sense, an uncanny knack to really assist people with their endeavors on route to huge successes. This means that her working career has ranged over the decades from an enthusiastic but naïve basketball coach to reaching the top levels of coaching across many sports and developing the first National and Higher national Diplomas in Sport Science when most people said it would never be possible. In essence, she conjures reality from what doesn't exist yet, and forges opportunities for the future in relation to, not only the young generations but for experienced adults looking for new vibrant pathways. She has created large health centres combining NHS with modern thoughts on health, helped change the landscape of pain management and truly put her heart and soul into reducing the reliance on opioids across the United Kingdom. Presently back working directly in her first love – professional sport, she is now humbly working towards flipping or understanding on how to look after athletes both on and off the field of play, joining the dots properly to prevent injury and take care of the players who are navigating their own journeys.

Paula reset by dedicating herself to her community clinics helping people with the usual aches and pains of life. It gives her purpose to know that she can assist people to be at work pain free and give their families and loved ones the best version of themselves.

Paula walks the walk with a large family of 3 adult children and is co-parent to two young ones. Two dogs and extended – everything. She lives life to the full in all aspects, enjoying the heat as much as her Icelandic life and can often be found wrapped in writing or reading. Paula's sneaky hobby is adventure and strategy games on the play station. This actually provides more skills sets than you can possibly imagine and has fun at the core. In all the spare hours she focused on fitness and strength, creating apps and planning future tours. In her words, "retirement is not a destination in career... change ...is. "

Contact: www.paulaessonclinic.com

Gerard Smith

Gerard is based in Co. Meath, Ireland. He is a full-time property investor/entrepreneur and has multiple properties globally. His area of interest is how businesses operate and finding new opportunities for his business and clients.

Contact: www.bluepropertyventures.com

LinkedIn: www.linkedin.com/in/gerard-smith-ireland

Heather Mortimer

Having become a single parent through marriage separation, Heather's main goal was to provide a bright and secure future for her children. With a "We still survive!" approach, she built her own company to make this possible.

She has since received several awards and recognitions for her business and its growth and has gone on to coach others to step up in business.

Her main focus is property, both in the UK and internationally. She is available for in-person and virtual coaching sessions, with Zoom groups and accountability sessions incorporated into her model.

Contact: www.lightbulbinternationalproperty.com

Natalie Duffy

Natalie Duffy is a qualified Social Worker from Derry. She is a mother to two children, Patrick Shea and Emily. Natalie's devotion is to her children and family. In her own time, Natalie enjoys studying Day Trading, attending investment workshops and developing her financial education.

Natalie has worked as a Social Worker for the last ten years and is dedicated to helping and supporting families during tough times. Natalie has faced many adversities throughout her life and at one stage, found herself at rock bottom. By facing her fears head on, she developed coping strategies and found a new outlook on life, that she hopes to share with the people she works with, with the goal of helping them overcome their adversities and improving their lives.

Natalie is now a big believer that consistency, dedication, and focus are the key to success and believes if you have the strength to change your mind, way of thinking and outlook, you can conquer anything.

Tanya Cannon

Tanya Cannon was born and raised in Athlone, County Westmeath. One of three siblings reared by a gorgeous mum and extended family, Tanya is director and owner of A1 Cleaning Services and Supplies. This highly professional, well-respected company employs over 50 local people and services a prestigious client base across the Midlands. Tanya had navigated many devastating challenges in her life, including profound domestic trauma and abuse, and a horrific sexual assault at the age of six. Never letting the traumas of her life hold her back, Tanya harnessed them as a catalyst for her determination to be successful, healthy and happy. She chooses every day to have a positive mindset, to be a passionate community member and to always share her generous nature in work and in her personal life. Instead of seeing negatives, Tanya sees opportunities to recognize gifts and potential, which in turn allow her to be a lighthouse for others, it has allowed her bright heart to shine. She is resilient and yet filled with joy and gratitude.

Tanya shows up every day with her infectious 'attitude of gratitude', inspiring others to make this world a better place.

Ian Jackson

Ian is a determined, creative and a resilient entrepreneur from County Down in Northern Ireland. The key to his success has been to invest in positive business relationships, knowing the market and knowing when to take the risk to move onto the next venture. Ian has been married to wife Gwen for 43 years, they have 4 children, and 3 grandchildren. He has invested greatly in inspiring his children and grandchildren to follow their entrepreneurial instincts.

Contact: www.jacksonandsonestates.com

Charles Eder

Charles Eder grew up in Europe, Africa, and the USA. From a small, adventurous, international family, Charles prides himself on his love of languages and the arts, business skills, and voluntary work. He has held many leadership roles in organizations and has started his own business with partners. He has won awards in public speaking, a bi-monthly current affairs show on radio, and business. Today, he spends his time working for one of the world's largest multi-national companies, travelling, and sourcing products and services. When he isn't reading a book, Charles is engaged discussing technology, the environment and best practices, playing chess, or improving cooking or other skills.

Ashleigh Tobin

Ashleigh Tobin helps clients get their MOJO* back through a reset of their health, their hormones, their head-game, and their habits. As an international award-winning speaker and a hormone health and mind coach, she draws on over 35 years' experience in the Irish health sector across nursing, conventional and complementary medicine, pharmaceuticals, coaching and mentoring to get real-life results.

'Kindness and Kick-A*s' is her mantra in both her one-to-one work and in her speaking engagements and workshops. Let's face it – we often know what we 'should' be doing but may need a bum-kick to make it happen.

Ashleigh delivers a pragmatic, frank, and fun message about thriving at every age by addressing issues such as low energy, sleep difficulties, poor motivation or stress which can be especially challenging during the perimenopause, menopause or andropause stages of life.

By combining an evidence-based, conventional medicine approach with the more holistic tools often needed to maintain a better work-life balance and deeper contentment in our everyday life, Ashleigh helps clients achieve a healthier, contented, values-driven life.

Ashleigh is a registered nurse, a licenced homoeopath, a Satir Coaching and Mentoring Specialist, a Master NLP practitioner and holds additional qualifications in Mind Coaching, Heartmath and CBT.

Living in Wicklow with her husband Eric, she enjoys walking, storytelling, Reformer Pilates, and gardening. You'll also find her riding pillion on the back of Eric's motorbike, ever since she's figured out how to pack everything into that very small motorbike pannier.

Contact: www.ashleightobin.com
https://linktr.ee/yourhormonehealth

Dawn Auchmuty

Dawn Auchmuty, a devoted Yoga & Pilates instructor, stylist and lover of wellness, hailing from the scenic shores of Galway, has always been guided by her unwavering passion for movement and music. From a tender age, she found solace and inspiration in the rhythm of melodies and the fluidity of motion, shaping her path towards a life enriched by creativity and self-discovery.

Immersing herself in the world of classical music for 12 years under the esteemed guidance of the Royal Irish Academy of Music, Dawn cultivated a profound appreciation for melody and rhythm, laying the foundation for her artistic journey. Alongside her musical pursuits, she eagerly delved into drama, ballet, contemporary dance, and singing in her home church choir, relishing every opportunity for creative expression.

With a career spanning over 15 years as a fashion stylist, Dawn discovered a unique platform to blend her love for creativity with her innate sense of style. From orchestrating captivating window displays to curating signature looks for her clients, she found boundless joy in helping others discover their own sense of fashion and self-expression. Driven by her love for the ocean and a curiosity for holistic wellness, Dawn delved into the practice of cold-water immersion, harnessing the power of breath to regulate the body and mind. Alongside her passion for outdoor pursuits like hiking, cycling, and running, Dawn finds solace and inspiration in the embrace of nature, recognising its profound ability to nourish and rejuvenate the soul. Yet, it was through her own journey to wellness, navigating life's trials and tribulations, that Dawn unearthed the transformative power of Yoga and Pilates. These practices became her sanctuary, offering healing on spiritual, physical, and emotional levels, igniting within her a fervent desire to share their benefits with others.

Dawn stands as a testament to the power of resilience, the beauty of love, and the transformative potential of adversity. Her story inspires others to embrace their own trials with courage, to find strength in vulnerability, and to discover the profound beauty that emerges from the depths of sorrow. Dawn infuses every aspect of her life with a deep reverence for wellness and holistic living. Through her teachings and offerings, she empowers her clients to embrace life fully, flourish in their pursuits, and nurture their wellbeing with grace and intention. She stands as a testament to her unwavering dedication to uplifting others on their path to wholeness and vitality.

Contact: www.instragram.com/aurora_sculpt_wellness

Shane Coyle

Shane Coyle is the owner of award-winning business SC PROPERTY SOURCING & INVESTMENTS.

He is an international property investor who began growing his property portfolio back in 2016 in Northern Ireland. He now offers his knowledge and experience to other investors that require some help and guidance as they are growing their portfolio. The priority for Shane's business is to ensure each of his clients can benefit from a full package service as they are building their empire. This would include everything from sourcing a suitable investment property, managing any renovation work and joint venture partnerships.

Shane has also recently expanded his services to offer property management for any short-term rental properties. This has led to the exciting launch of TRAVEL LETS in 2024. www.travel-lets.com Travelling, exploring and creating memories with his family is where his passion lies. In his spare time Shane likes to go swimming, play golf and go to the gym. He is a newspaper columnist for The

Strabane Herald and likes to keep the readers up to date on all thing's property investing.

If you would like to get in touch, you can find Shane on all social media platforms under 'Shane Coyle Property'

Contact: www.scpropertysourcingandinvestments.com
shane@scpropertysourcingandinvestments.com

Have Courage

At the edge of possibility, where paths begin to weave,

Decision awaits your courage, a future to conceive.

The crossroads of your life, with options spread so wide,

The journey of a thousand miles begins with but a stride.

Embrace the unknown journey, let hesitation fade,

Every single decision shapes the world you've made.

Within your heart lies wisdom, a compass tried and true,

Trust your intuition, it knows what you must do.

The power of decision lies deep within your core,

Every choice, each brave embrace, can open a new door.

Stand tall, be a victor, let your confidence rise.

With every heartbeat, every breath the answers you will find.

A world of endless wonders awaits your willing hand,

Step forward into greatness, where bold decisions stand.

The gateway to your potential, where all adventures meet,

Know within the heart of hearts that decision makes you complete.

Live FULLY!

Donna Kennedy Slattery

FOR MORE INFORMATION, BOOKS AND EVENTS

GO TO

WWW.DONNAKENNEDY.COM

Printed in France by Amazon
Brétigny-sur-Orge, FR

21736453R00178